TEACHING MATERIALS FOR COLLEGE STUDENTS
高等学校教材

U0795433

Society and Culture of Oil-producing Countries

产油国社会与文化

主编　淳柳　王艳

中国石油大学出版社
CHINA UNIVERSITY OF PETROLEUM PRESS
山东·青岛

图书在版编目(CIP)数据

产油国社会与文化 / 淳柳,王艳主编 . -- 青岛:
中国石油大学出版社,2023. 3

ISBN 978-7-5636-7677-4

Ⅰ. ①产… Ⅱ. ①淳…②王… Ⅲ. ①石油生产国—
概况—世界 Ⅳ. ①F416. 22

中国国家版本馆 CIP 数据核字(2023)第 033973 号

中国石油大学(华东)规划教材

书　　名:产油国社会与文化
CHANYOUGUO SHEHUI YU WENHUA

主　　编:淳柳　王艳

责任编辑:隋芳(电话　0532-86983568)

封面设计:王凌波

出 版 者:中国石油大学出版社
(地址:山东省青岛市黄岛区长江西路 66 号　邮编:266580)

网　　址:http://cbs.upc.edu.cn

电子邮箱:shiyoujiaoyu@126.com

排 版 者:青岛友一广告传媒有限公司

印 刷 者:泰安市成辉印刷有限公司

发 行 者:中国石油大学出版社(电话　0532-86983437)

开　　本:787 mm × 1 092 mm　1/16

印　　张:8.75

字　　数:276 千字

版 印 次:2023 年 3 月第 1 版　2023 年 3 月第 1 次印刷

书　　号:ISBN 978-7-5636-7677-4

定　　价:22.00 元

PREFACE

前 言

长期以来,行业化办学与专业化培养作为我国高校办学的基本形式,曾为国家培养了大批急需人才。但随着社会的发展,高度专业化的培养模式开始呈现出明显的局限性,培养出的人才素质与现代社会的要求存在较大差距。2017年以来,教育部积极推进"新工科"建设,旨在培养造就一大批多样化、创新型卓越工程科技人才,为我国产业发展和国际竞争提供智力和人才支撑,这既是当务之急,也是长远之策。"新工科"高等教育需培养学生具备过硬的专业技能,同时全面提升其人文素养。在此背景下,通识教育理念在我国高校内外已经得到较为普遍的认可,通识课程则是实现通识教育理念的主要载体和渠道。《产油国社会与文化》教材基于中国石油大学(华东)"世界主要产油国文化概论"这门通识课程多年来的教学实践编写而成,面向石油类院校本科生。本教材有利于探索"新工科"背景下专业特色优势与人文素养能力培养的有机融合,在提升学生英语语言技能的同时,拓宽其人文学科知识。

党的二十大提出"推进文化自信自强,铸就社会主义文化新辉煌"。文化强国的内涵就是发展面向现代化、面向世界、面向未来的,民族的科学的大众的社会主义文化。其中,面向世界指的是在中华文化走出去的同时,吸纳人类文明优秀成果。世界上姹紫嫣红的各国文化都扎根于自己生存的土壤,凝聚着一个国家、一个民族的非凡智慧和精神追求。文明因交流而多彩,文化因互鉴而丰富。作为当今世界的主要能源之一,石油是人类文明进步的重要物质基础和动力,关系国计民生和国家安全。坚持实施更大范围、更宽领域、更深层次的对外开放,开拓能源国际合作新局面是我国"十四五"能源体系规划的基本原则之一。通过对产油国社会文化的学习与探究,可帮助学生了解产油国基本概况,培养他们的跨文化交际能力与批判性思维能力,帮助他们建立起更加均衡的知识体系、良好的认知结构与敏锐的思维习惯,为开拓能源国际市场、提高行业竞争力打下坚实基础,有效对接国家能源发展战略对高层次人才的紧急需求。

本教材根据中国之外的世界主要产油国所在区域划分为六个章节，分别介绍中东、独联体、非洲、拉美、北美与北欧、东南亚等区域产油国的社会与文化。每章围绕该区域产油国社会与文化诸方面精选素材，内容涉及区域社会与文化共性、国别社会与文化特色，兼顾社会与文化的历史传承和现代创新。教学素材来源多样，涵盖相关区域联盟、各国政府、能源组织等官网上有关产油国社会与文化的真实语料，以及 BBC、National Geographic、TED 等多媒体平台和影视剧作品中有关产油国社会与文化的纪录片和视频节选，保证了教材内容的多元化与权威性。

在教学内容安排上，每章根据循序渐进的原则分为三个部分：第一部分简要介绍各区域社会与文化的整体概况，通过设置视听说多模态学习任务，使课程更加生动、直观，符合当代大学生的认知心理；第二部分选取该区域三个产油国，通过篇章阅读帮助学生进一步了解其社会与文化诸方面的内容，文后辅以相关词汇练习、知识点问答、长难句翻译、思辨性讨论与主题拓展写作等，旨在强化学生的英语语言技能、提升其人文素养；第三部分聚焦跨文化交际真实情景，立足学生未来职业发展需求，为其提供有益的参考和借鉴。

本书的整体策划和审定者为淳柳，负责全书统筹、前言撰写以及第一章、第三章和第六章的编写工作，共计撰写 14.1 万字；王艳负责本书第二章、第四章和第五章的编写工作，共计撰写 13.5 万字。两位主编均具有丰富的产油国社会与文化教学及研究经验。

本教材的编写得到“中国石油大学（华东）规划教材项目”及“山东省研究生教育质量提升计划项目”专项资金的支持，在此特别致谢！外交部外语专家陈明明先生、中国石油大学（华东）石油工程学院任韶然教授对教材进行了审读并提出了诸多建设性修订建议，创造太阳能源服务（青岛）有限公司联合创始人官智武先生、中国石油工程建设有限公司中东地区公司采购部经理王维先生基于长期驻外工作经历多次为本教材的编写提供专业指导，外国语言文学专业硕士研究生王紫梦和油气田开发工程专业博士研究生 Seyed Behzad Saberali 承担了部分资料的检索与核查工作，在此深表谢意！同时，真诚感谢中国石油大学出版社和编辑老师对教材的审读与反馈！

本教材使用方便，读者可以选择自己感兴趣的任何区域或国家进行学习，在短时间内即可了解其社会与文化的概况和特色，并寻求到相应的跨文化交际与沟通建议。由于涉及知识面广，加之作者水平有限，教材中不妥之处在所难免，恳请广大师生提出宝贵意见与建议，以便不断修改完善。

编　者

2022 年 12 月

CONTENTS

目　录

Unit 1　Oil-producing Countries in the Middle East ········· **1**

Overview ········· 1

Text A　Visiting Riyadh: A Look at Saudi Arabia's Social and Cultural Transformations ········· 4

Text B　What Is a "Tarof"? — The Persian Art of Etiquette ········· 10

Text C　United Arab Emirates at a Glance ········· 15

Practical Tips ········· 19

Unit 2　Oil-producing Countries in the Commonwealth of Independent States ········· **22**

Overview ········· 22

Text A　The Great Silk Road in Kazakhstan ········· 26

Text B　Orthodox Churches in Russia ········· 32

Text C　Intangible Cultural Heritage of Azerbaijan ········· 37

Practical Tips ········· 42

Unit 3　Oil-producing Countries in Africa ········· **47**

Overview ········· 47

Text A　Emergence of Nigeria as a Political and Economic Entity ········· 51

Text B　Discover Algeria in a Nutshell ········· 55

Text C　Ancient Egyptian Civilization ········· 60

Practical Tips ········· 66

Unit 4 Oil-producing Countries in Latin America ······ **71**

Overview ······ 71

Text A How Soccer Came to Define Brazil ······ 74

Text B Day of the Dead in Mexico ······ 79

Text C Hyperinflation in Venezuela ······ 83

Practical Tips ······ 87

Unit 5 Oil-producing Countries in North America and Northern Europe ······ **92**

Overview ······ 92

Text A Canadian Icons and Emblems ······ 95

Text B Why Is Norway So Good at the Winter Games? ······ 101

Text C Oil Production of Canada and America ······ 105

Practical Tips ······ 110

Unit 6 Oil-producing Countries in Southeast Asia ······ **114**

Overview ······ 114

Text A Approaching Indonesia ······ 117

Text B The Diversity of Malaysia ······ 122

Text C Confucianism in Vietnam ······ 128

Practical Tips ······ 131

UNIT 1

Oil-producing Countries in the Middle East

Overview

The Middle East is a transcontinental region. The term has come into wider usage as a replacement of the term Near East (as opposed to the Far East) beginning in the early 20th century. Arabs, Turks, Persians, Kurds, and Azeris (excluding Azerbaijan) constitute the largest ethnic groups in the region by population. Several major religions have their origins in the Middle East, including Judaism, Christianity, and Islam. The Middle East generally has a hot, arid climate, with several major rivers providing irrigation to support agriculture in limited areas such as the Nile Delta in Egypt, the Tigris and Euphrates watersheds of Mesopotamia, and most of what is known as the Fertile Crescent. Throughout its history, the Middle East has been a major center of world affairs, a strategically, economically, politically, culturally, and religiously sensitive area.

Task 1 Topic discussion.

How do you understand the last sentence of the above paragraph? Please give some examples to explain it.

____

____

____

____

____

Task 2 Listen to the following recording and then fill in the blanks. ①

Even as the Omicron version of the coronavirus spreads, camel owners from Bahrain, Kuwait, Oman, Saudi Arabia and Qatar recently traveled to the United Arab Emirates. They brought with them 40,000 of their most beautiful camels for the Al Dhafra Festival, an event that celebrates desert culture. Camel beauty is decided based on appearances agreed upon generations ago. Only female camels take part because males fight too much, experts said.

A five-man jury decides the winners. One of the organizers, Mohammed al-Muhari, described what 1__________ were looking for as hundreds of camels were being shown. Necks must be long and thin, cheeks wide and hooves large, he told the Associated Press. Lips must hang down. The camels must walk tall. "It's not so different from humans," al-Muhari said. Some breeders have tried to cheat. They use banned 2__________ to grow the camel's lips, soften the face and increase the size of the camel's back. Festival spokesman Abdel Hadi Saleh would not say how many breeders had been banned over measures to change a camel's 3__________. All camels have detailed medical examinations before entering Al Dhafra Festival. Since Emirati investigators began using X-rays and other devices a few years ago, Saleh said the number of cheaters has fallen. "We easily catch them, and they realize getting caught, it's not worth the cost to their 4__________," he said.

A great deal is at stake. Al Dhafra Festival offers the top 10 winners in each category prizes from $1,300 to $13,600. At the main Saudi contest, the most beautiful get high prices. Camels change hands in deals worth millions of dirhams, a local form of money. But breeders say it is not only about the money. Saleh al-Minhali is a camel-owner from Dubai. "It is a kind of our 5__________ and custom that the Emirati rulers revived," he said.

Revive is a term that means to bring back. Gone are the days when camels were important for daily life in the country. However, experts say Emiratis are increasingly searching for 6__________. This includes Bedouin traditions that were common before the UAE became a nation 50 years ago. Rima Sabban of the Zayed University in Dubai said, "Younger Emiratis who have identity issues are going back to their heritage to find 7__________."

Sabban added, "The society developed and modernized so fast. It creates a crisis inside."

Festivals across the country celebrate 8______________________________. Al Dhafra also features falcon racing, camel dancing and a camel milking contest. Each category in the 10-day contest is divided into two types of camels: Mahaliyat, the tan breed that comes from the UAE and Oman, and Majaheen, the darker breed from Saudi Arabia. For hours, judges studied each camel, writing lists of the animals' body parts for scoring purposes. Breeders shouted to surprise camels so 9______________________________. As the sun set over the sands, the

① The audio can be accessed here: https://www.51voa.com/VOA_Special_English/in-the-uae-a-camel-contest-celebrates-desert-culture-88196.html.

winning breeders were called to accept their prizes. Camels were crowned with gold and silver-lined cloth. "We've received over 40 prizes in various camel contests this year alone," said Mohammed Saleh bin Migrin al-Amri as he held four from the day, including two golds. After that, he jumped into his vehicle and 10________________________.

Task 3 Watch the TED talk titled *A Saudi, an Indian and an Iranian walk into a Qatari bar...* and answer the following questions. ①

Brief introduction to the speech: Iranian-American comedian Maz Jobrani takes to the TEDxSummit stage in Doha, Qatar to take on "serious issues" in the Middle East.

1. When people from Middle East see each other, how many kisses are they going to give?

____

____

2. Which way of greeting is not suggested on an American airplane according to the speaker?

____

____

Task 4 Understand Middle East through film.

American East is a 2008 American drama film about Arab-Americans living in Los Angeles after the September 11 attack. The story examines long-held misunderstandings about Arabic and Islamic culture, and puts a human face on a segment of the American population about whom most Americans know nothing, but who today are of particular interest to them, either from curiosity or suspicion.

Please answer the following questions after seeing the film.

1. How do you understand the name of the film?

____

____

2. What are the long-held misunderstandings about Arabic and Islamic culture?

____

____

① The video can be accessed here: https://www.ted.com/talks/maz_jobrani_a_saudi_an_indian_and_an_iranian_walk_into_a_qatari_bar.

Lead in

There is no accurate conclusion on which countries and regions Middle East includes. It generally refers to West Asia and North Africa. The terms "Middle East" and "oil-rich" are often taken as synonyms of each other. The oil-producing countries mainly include Saudi Arabia, Iran, Iraq, United Arab Emirates (UAE), Kuwait, Qatar, Oman, Yemen and Syria (see Figure 1-1) .

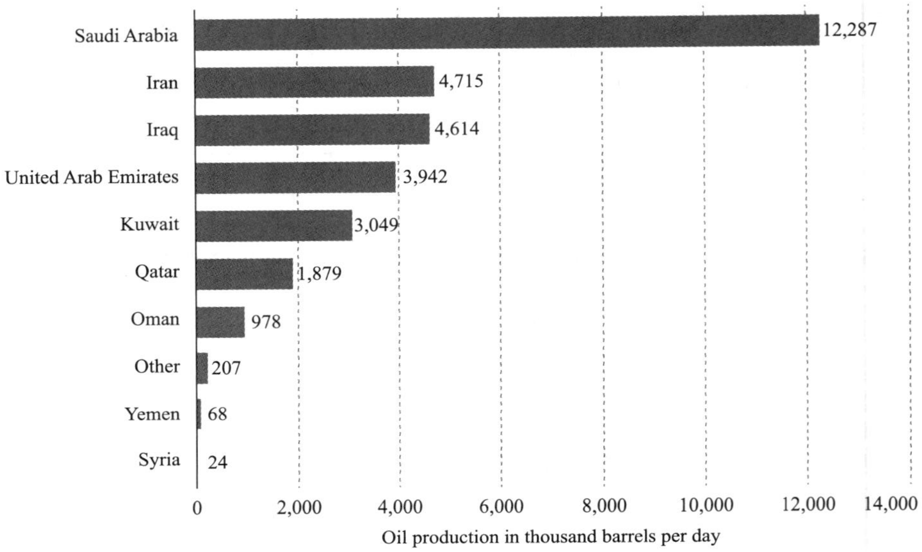

Figure 1-1 Oil-producing Countries in the Middle East[①]

Text A

Visiting Riyadh: A Look at Saudi Arabia's Social and Cultural Transformations[②]

The Kingdom of Saudi Arabia is undergoing several social, economic, and cultural changes. As it pivots towards an increasingly national, rather than religious identity, government investments

① Oil Production in the Middle East in 2018, by Country. (2022-03-28)[2022-08-21]. https://www.statista.com/statistics/218302/oil-production-in-key-middle-eastern-countries/.

② CUSTERS D. Visiting Riyadh: A Look at Saudi Arabia's Social and Cultural Transformations. (2022-03-25)[2022-05-02]. https://www.stimson.org/2022/visiting-riyadh-a-look-at-saudi-arabias-social-and-cultural-transformations/.

are being made in promoting contemporary and historical Saudi culture as well as the kingdom's history as a nation. Furthermore, the kingdom is investing in its economic growth, among others through increased job opportunities for Saudi nationals.

Its capital city, Riyadh, has become a site where these changes are particularly visible, among others through the government investments in cultural heritage restoration and the city's infrastructure. This field note describes some of the changes taking place as observed by its author in her recent visit to the kingdom, and asks who, though many support the changes, are the losers of the developments taking place.

After two years of limited travel due to the Covid-19 pandemic, I was finally able to visit the Kingdom of Saudi Arabia within the context of my work as a Research Associate for the Stimson Center's Middle East and North Africa Program. I was very curious to meet with Saudis and hear firsthand about the changes the kingdom has gone through in the last few years. In this field note, I will share some of the impressions made during my short visit.

Cultural change: literature and heritage

One of my personal passions is literature. So naturally, when traveling to Saudi Arabia, I was keen to learn about the literary scene in the kingdom. From my previous research, I know that Saudi Arabia, as well as the Gulf at large, has seen an increasing literary output. Historically, the country has been at the periphery of literary production, especially when it comes to novels and short stories. But in the last decade literary output has grown. Noticeable in this respect is the increased government institutional support and investment in culture and the role technology and social media play in making access to and distribution of literature easier.

When it comes to this latter, I met one Saudi who mentioned the phenomenon of "Twitter poetry", where people are sharing their poetry and short-short stories on Twitter, rather than having them published through the traditional channels. Furthermore, technology has made it easier for those interested in literature to for example get together online through book clubs.

When it comes to government support for culture and arts, Saudi Arabia established the Ministry of Culture in 2018. Culture, according to the Saudi 2030 vision, is indispensable to the quality of life, and thus the kingdom aims to increase both the quality and quantity of its cultural activities. The Ministry, among others, supports literary production and translation, but also cultural events and the development and restoration of Saudi heritage.

One example of this latter is the al-Turaif district in ad-Dariyah, which I was pleased to visit. This site, the original home of the Saudi royal family, is built in the unique Najdi architectural style and was declared a UNESCO site in 2010. A second example, which I visited, is that of Saudi's first contemporary art Biennale, organized by the Diriyah Biennale

Foundation, where contemporary art from inside and outside of the kingdom was shown.

Arts: maintaining the past for the future

These examples show the increased cultural developments in Saudi Arabia, though some question the speed with which it is taking place. One artist I met mentioned that the change towards modernization in the art world was going too fast and elaborated that there were many new artists who had not studied art and were producing just for the sake of producing. They described an increasingly developing market-oriented art scene, which despite its potential positive consequences, could also be to the detriment of quality art.

During my trip I purchased an original artwork by Lama Al-Mugbel, a Saudi art student, at a calligraphy exhibition at the Princess Nourah Bint Abdulrahman University. I found that her print combined traditional elements of art, such as calligraphy, with a modern technique. The print shows the Kaaba in Mecca, and to me, it symbolizes somehow a contemporary perception of what Saudi Arabia is, and a projection of the kingdom's history into the future.

Saudi Arabia's changing identity: from a religious to a national identity

The developments in Saudi Arabia's cultural scene are both focused on increasing the awareness of the Saudi public on its history as a nation, as well as part of the Saudi initiative to attract more international tourism. Concerning the latter, it has become very easy to apply for a Saudi tourism visa. Something that took weeks to arrange is now achieved in a few minutes.

Linked to these developments is another theme I often heard during my visit, namely the shift of Saudi Arabia from a country with a religious identity historically linked to Wahhabism, to a national identity in which all Saudis are included. This shift was made clear in an interview Crown Prince Mohammed Bin Salman gave recently.

This new Saudi national identity is also accompanied by reforms when it comes to discrimination, yet, as one Saudi I met shared, this is still happening. In the meantime, the religious sphere has become less unreachable. Clerics have become more approachable as they are increasingly taking to Twitter and other social media and are engaging with the Saudi public directly.

Riyadh: the city of Saudi Arabia's future

Unfortunately, my visit to Saudi Arabia was limited to the capital city Riyadh. During many of my meetings, the city-rural divide in Saudi Arabia became clear when it came to social and economic change. Riyadh is the capital of this change, but that does not mean it will trickle down to rural areas. Nevertheless, the Saudi government developed a plan to make the city one of the world's most important. This includes increasing the number of its inhabitants to 15–20 million, growth to be achieved among others through economic possibilities.

The government works to provide many incentives for the growth of the city, such as increased opportunities for Saudi nationals to work in the private and public sectors through the Nitaqat framework. Riyadh is also becoming more pleasurable to live in. For example, I could see the work on the large metro network being built that should make transport through the city easier. Furthermore, several nature areas in and around Riyadh have been restored, such as Wadi Hanifa, which nowadays Saudis go to on the weekends.

Conclusion: inclusive social change

Many of the people I met support the changes taking place. Being cautious of the caveat of generalization, this supportive group included many Western-educated young people who chose to come back to the kingdom and are now working together to build up their future. Yet, I also heard several times that not enough is done when it comes to the rights of women and minorities.

Caution is furthermore in place not to assume the recent developments benefit all, as economic growth and social change always come with losers. During my visit to Saudi Arabia, it was not clear to me who they are, though I had some thoughts. Could they be the migrant workers who came to Saudi Arabia? Or the citizens who are losing their homes to make way for new development projects? Or others who remain invisible? Thus, though I heard many positive stories about the recent developments, from the cultural sector to the increased economic opportunities and standard of living in Riyadh, time will tell how sustainable the developments are from a social point of view.

Exercises

Task 1 Decide whether the following sentences are True or False.

1. Riyadh has become a site where changes are particularly visible. ( )
2. Historically, Saudi Arabia has been at the center of literary production, especially when it comes to novels and short stories. ( )
3. In order to support culture and arts, the government established the Ministry of Culture in 2016. ( )
4. The increasingly developing market-oriented art scene has both advantages and disadvantages. ( )
5. The author was allowed to visit any place in Saudi Arabia. ( )

Task 2 Answer the following questions according to the information from text A.

1. As it pivots towards an increasingly national, rather than religious identity, which fields are the government investments being made in?

____

____

2. What is "Twitter poetry"?

____

____

3. Why have clerics become more approachable in Saudi Arabia nowadays?

____

____

4. Which framework helped to provide increased opportunities for Saudi nationals to work in the private and public sectors?

____

____

5. What does the last sentence of this text imply?

____

____

Task 3 Translate the following sentences into Chinese.

1. I was very curious to meet with Saudis and hear firsthand about the changes the kingdom has gone through in the last few years.

____

____

2. Noticeable in this respect is the increased government institutional support and investment in culture and the role technology and social media play in making access to and distribution of literature easier.

____

____

3. The developments in Saudi Arabia's cultural scene are both focused on increasing the awareness of the Saudi public on its history as a nation, as well as part of the Saudi initiative to attract more international tourism.

____

____

Task 4 Critical thinking enhancement.

Saudi Arabia's Vision 2030, launched in 2016, is a robust economic development framework to diversify the Saudi economy and make it the Arab and Islamic world heart, global investment power and the hub among Asia, Europe and Africa. The Arab diversification visions were probably inspired by the late Saudi energy minister Sheikh Yamani, who famously said in 2000, "The Stone Age didn't end for lack of stone, and the Oil Age will end long before the world runs out of oil." How do you understand the last sentence?

____

____

____

____

____

Text B

What Is a "Tarof"? — The Persian Art of Etiquette①

If anyone wants to understand a country and its people, they should start by knowing and understanding their culture and customs. Tarof (Taarof or Ta'arof) is an old Persian tradition and the Iranian art of etiquette. Anthropologists trace the origins of tarof to an Arabic word meaning "acquaintance" or "knowledge". Like many Arabic words that have found their way into the Persian language, tarof has been transformed into something uniquely Iranian. It is about raising others and "self-lowering" which is the sign of respect. Iranian hospitality is more than just being polite. Iranians are known for being one of the most hospitable people in the world.

Persian hospitality

From the very young age, Iranian kids are taught to share their toys with friends and save their candies or sweets for them because guests are important people. It comes from the Persian tradition of putting your guests and their need first and the insatiable desire to be the best hosts. Iranians always go to extreme length to provide the best of everything they have for their guests. There is often more food offered to you than you can eat. Part of Iranian hospitality is showering the guests with abundance even when they have financial problems.

William O. Beeman, the linguistic anthropologist at the University of Minnesota says the idea of tarof is to abase oneself while exalting the other person. He explains tarof as "fighting for the lower hand", but in an exquisitely elegant way, making it possible, in a hierarchical society like Iran's, "for people to paradoxically deal with each other as equals".

Explaining the concept of tarof is a bit complicated especially to the people that never experienced that. So we'd better start by giving examples.

A simple example of tarof is when two friends or colleagues want to enter or leave the room. Usually anywhere in the world in this situation one of them says "after you" and then they enter the room. But that's not the case in Iran. They keep "tarofing" and complimenting each other till finally one of them gives up and enters first and even then he would say "sorry"! The person who forces the other to go through the door first is being graceful and has shown deference to the other person.

---

① What Is a "Tarof"? — The Persian Art of Etiquette. (2019-04-30) [2022-03-12]. http://www.persiansarenotarabs.com/persian-tarof/.
PARVINI S. Great Read: In the Persian World of "Ta'arof", They Make Offers That Will Be Refused. (2015-07-06)[2022-03-12]. https://www.latimes.com/local/great-reads/la-me-c1-tarof-20150706-story.html.

Sitting with your back to someone is considered extremely rude in Persian culture. But on some occasions you have to. That's when tarof comes handy. Imagine you're sitting in the front seat of a car, you should immediately apologize and say "Bebakhshid Poshtam be shomast" literally meaning "sorry my back is to you". The tarof continues as the person behind you says "Gol posht o rou nadar e" which means "a flower has no front or back". So the person behind you is calling you a flower, at this point either you say "thank you" or further compliment the one in the back seat by saying "Posht e gol bagh e gol e" meaning "behind the flower is the garden of flower". You're basically saying "he is a garden"! So in the end no one is offended.

Tarof — at the party

If you're invited to an Iranian household for the first time, bring flower or a box of chocolate. When the host says "thank you" and "chera zahmat keshidid" meaning something like "why did you do it", you could say "ghabel e shoma ro nadar e" meaning "it's not worthy of you". You should check to see if the host is wearing shoes. If not, remove yours at the door.

In an Iranian house usually you're supposed to take off your shoes before entering the house. It would be considered rude to walk on the precious Persian carpet with your shoes on. It's also very polite to greet the elders first. Shaking hands with the children and praising their politeness is also appreciated.

At the party if you are offered something like beverages or food, you are supposed to refuse at first so you won't come out as greedy or impolite. The host then would insist and offer again and finally you would accept it. When you're leaving the party, you should say to the host "bebakhshid zahmat dadam" which means "sorry for causing you trouble" even though you are invited to the party. Any other scenario would be considered rude. Then the host would literally beg you to stay for the night or a bit more, even if it is 2 in the morning or the host is exhausted. In that case, you're supposed to politely decline.

Tarof — paying for the restaurant bill

If you see two Iranians arguing in a restaurant, don't panic; they're probably fighting over who is going to pay the bill. Everyone will try to pay the bill even by snatching credit card out of your hand. But don't worry if you don't get to pay this time; things will even out as you treat someone next time and vice versa.

Tarof — complimenting something

If you praise anything in an Iranian household, they would offer it to you even if it's very valuable. If you compliment Iranians for their look, they won't answer by simply saying "thank you". They say "cheshmatoon ghashang mibin e" which literally means "your eyes see it beautifully".

Tarof — in a taxi

It is common for Persian taxi drivers to tell you "ghabel nadir e" at the end of the ride when you're trying to pay the fare. Out of respect they refuse at first but eventually take the money. There is an unwritten rule of two or three rounds of offering and refusing. Also Iranian taxi drivers usually start a chat with their passengers about social or political issues and you'd be surprised how informed they are.

Tarof — in the shop

Tarof is also a big part of the buying and selling in Persian culture. When you ask an Iranian shop keeper the price of the item you're going to buy, the seller first refuses and says "ghabel e shoma ro nadar e", then you say "khahesh mikonam" meaning "please, I insist". Next, the shop keeper replies "mehman e man bashid" meaning "be my guest" and finally tells you the price.

In a culture that emphasizes deference, tarof is a verbal dance that circles around respect. Whether they're 8 or 80 years old, whether they're Muslim, Jewish, Christian, Zoroastrian — it doesn't matter. If they're Persian, they probably practice some form of tarof.

Exercises

Task 1 Please list the different situations where tarof is employed according to text B.

____

____

____

____

____

Task 2 Answer the following questions according to the information from text B.

1. What is tarof according to William O. Beeman?

____

____

2. What are the expected steps of showing tarof when you have to sit with your back to someone?

____

____

3. What are the similarities and differences between Iranian tarof and Chinese *limao*?

____

____

Task 3 Translate the following sentences into Chinese.

1. Like many Arabic words that have found their way into the Persian language, tarof has been transformed into something uniquely Iranian.

____

____

2. But don't worry if you don't get to pay this time; things will even out as you treat someone next time and vice versa.

____

____

3. Also Iranian taxi drivers usually start a chat with their passengers about social or political issues and you'd be surprised how informed they are.

____

____

Task 4 Please write an essay of 300 words about the ancient Persian culture.

There was a time when the ancient Persian civilization was, in fact, the most powerful empire in the world, which was known for its military strength and wise rulers. The following documentary may be helpful for your writing.

IRAN, The Forgotten Glory is the first independent documentary film series taking the audience on a journey into the depths of ancient Persian civilization, capturing the majesty and the splendor of the Achaemenid and Sassanid empires and their influence on world history, religion, art and culture by revealing the ancient tales hidden in the ruins and reliefs which exist today as a testament to their legacy.

Text C

United Arab Emirates at a Glance①

The United Arab Emirates, often referred to as the UAE, is a federation of seven emirates on the eastern side of the Arabian Peninsula, at the entrance to the Persian Gulf. In less than four decades, the nation has transformed from a tribal culture reliant on agriculture and fishing to an entrepreneurial success story with world-class infrastructure. Powered largely (but no means exclusively) by oil wealth, the UAE today is defined by opulent resort hotels, ultra-modern architecture and a seemingly unending thirst for new and innovative mega-projects.

History

It can be fascinating to examine the UAE's foray into the modern world when only decades ago, the country was occupied by desert roaming, nomadic Bedouin tribes, who enjoyed simple existences in fishing villages and the peaceful, expansive desert. The Bedouin people traded with merchants from Iran, China and India before the arrival of Europeans in the 1400s. From the late 1400s, the Portuguese had control over much of the coastal emirates. But in an 1892 treaty, the sheiks that had control over what we now know as the UAE gave up much of their foreign relations power to the British government.

Trading of the UAE's "black gold" (crude oil) — the source of the country's infallible wealth — commenced in 1962, after years of hardship that followed the downfall of the pearling industry in the 1930s. The 1892 treaty ended in 1971 and the Persian Gulf sheikdoms began negotiations to form a union of Arab emirates. On 2 December 1971, Abu Dhabi and Dubai joined forces with other emirates to form the United Arab Emirates. Sheikh Zayed bin Sultan Al Nahyan, the former ruler of Abu Dhabi, became the UAE's first president.

Culture

The Emirati culture has been shaped through the centuries by two distinct communities. Along the coast the pearling industry and sea trading were the biggest influences in the way the people lived, while inland the Bedouins carried on with farming and looking after the date palms. Although the two subcultures were involved in vastly different industries they shared political, social and economical views and this brought them together.

---

① The United Arab Emirates. [2022-03-18]. http://www.uaecd.org/uae-introduction.
United Arab Emirates History, Language and Culture. (2017-03-12) [2022-03-18]. https://www.worldtravelguide.net/guides/middle-east/united-arab-emirates/history-language-culture/.

The lifestyle of the Arab tribes was dictated to according to the terrain they lived in but whether it was desert or coast it was a harsh environment. The people had to be resilient and resourceful and learn to make the best of what they had.

Unlike nowadays when families scatter far and wide across the globe, the traditions of family obligations were strong. Families lived and worked together with the more able bodied looking after an extended family of young, old and infirm relatives. A selfless individual in the tribe was seen to have pride and honour.

The combination of Emirati Arab culture mixed with Southeast and South Asian as well as African and other immigrants who live here adds to an already vast and vibrant melting pot of cultures. With such a cosmopolitan mix of people the UAE has an incredibly diverse culture but still retains strong Arab and Islamic influences. This is reflected everywhere in the music, cuisine, attire and architecture.

To keep the heritage and culture of the UAE alive in this fast changing world there are different events throughout the year such as camel races, dhow races and longboat races organized by the Emirates Heritage Club. Other events such as lectures, exhibitions and theatrical displays are all arranged to encourage an interest in this young country with a very ancient history.

Introduced to the area in 640 AD, Islam is the main religion but there are Hindu temples, mosques, churches and Sikh Gurdwara as the Emiratis are very tolerant of other religions. The holiest day of the week for Muslims is Friday and it is always part of their weekend. The scattering of mosques round the country means the Muslims are called to prayer five times a day by the sound of the adhan coming from the minarets. The end of Ramadan is celebrated by a national holiday called Eid ul-Fitr or Feast of Breaking the Fast. After 29 or 30 days of fasting from dawn to sunset, a special Eid prayer is said and then visits are made to friends and family to wish them well.

Emirati nationals account for about 11% of the population of around 8 million. The largest group to make up the UAE society are South Asians from India, Bangladesh and Pakistan who outnumber other Arabs by nearly two to one. Western expats only make up a very small proportion of the population. UAE society has changed to keep up with the needs of this mix of nationalities that have arrived over the years and international schools, themed restaurants and shops selling western clothing are to be found in certain areas throughout the country. The most obvious change to society in the UAE has been brought about by the sudden wealth to the country and the effects of expat culture. The more positive aspects of better schooling, hospitals, work and education for women are just a few of the major changes that the Arabs have benefited from in recent times. As with all good things there are some downsides. The divorce rates are higher, obesity is becoming a problem and some of the traditional family values are being lost in this mad whirlwind of advancement and technology.

Social conventions

The UAE is an Islamic country and women may feel more comfortable when dressed modestly. Even though foreign women can dress as they please, covering the shoulders and knees is a requirement in public areas like shopping centers and also during periods of religious significance. Men are also expected to dress with respect. Homosexuality and adultery are both illegal and while non-married couples aren't lawfully permitted to stay together in the same hotel room, it is common practice and rarely enforced.

Alcohol is tolerated, with non-Muslims allowed to drink alcohol in the cities' plentiful hotel bars and restaurants (except for Sharjah). Young people under 20s are not allowed to drink alcohol or buy cigarettes. It is illegal for everyone to eat, drink or smoke in public during daylight hours of the holy month of Ramadan, and on the day or eve of days of national importance, alcohol isn't sold and bars are shut. As in all Islamic countries, it's best to keep displays of affection private — kissing or embracing in public is not only considered disrespectful, it could lead to police caution or even arrest. Holding hands is generally fine, but swearing, rude gestures and drink driving are all punishable by imprisonment. Drugs are a strict no-no and could land you in serious trouble. It's worth checking what medicine and painkillers you bring into the country, as even some common pain medications like codeine are prohibited.

Exercises

Task 1 Answer the following questions according to the information from text C.

1. Why does the UAE have an incredibly diverse culture?

____

____

2. What events are held in order to keep the heritage and culture of the UAE alive in this fast changing world?

____

____

3. What are the downsides in UAE recently?

____

____

Task 2 Translate the following sentences into Chinese.

1. In less than four decades, the nation has transformed from a tribal culture reliant on agriculture and fishing to an entrepreneurial success story with world-class infrastructure.

____

____

2. Trading of the UAE's "black gold" (crude oil) — the source of the country's infallible wealth — commenced in 1962, after years of hardship that followed the downfall of the pearling industry in the 1930s.

____

____

3. The most obvious change to society in the UAE has been brought about by the sudden wealth to the country and the effects of expat culture.

____

____

Task 3 Expanded learning: *Abu Dhabi, Oil-Rich Capital of the UAE.*①

Abu Dhabi is the capital city of the United Arab Emirates. This modern seaside city is a perfect interpretation of what can be called "low-key luxury". Built with an investment of nearly USD $3 billion, the Emirates Palace is known as one of the world's premier seven-star resorts. The top floor features luxury suites reserved for royalty and heads of state. The modern Louvre Abu Dhabi has countless treasures on display. The magnificent Sheikh Zayed Grand Mosque is like a grand white palace with beautiful interior decoration. The Abu Dhabi Corniche is a beautiful seaside promenade from which visitors can appreciate the city's charm. This is a unique landscape not only for the stunning sea view but also the forest of skyscrapers that stand next to it. Try to discover the real Abu Dhabi with the guidance of this video.

____

____

____

____

____

① The video can be accessed here: https://www.bilibili.com/video/BV11K4y1C7jG?spm_id_from=333.337.search-card.all.click.

Practical Tips

Business Etiquette in the Middle East[①]

Meeting and greeting

Status is important and must be recognized by using the correct title when addressing someone. It is customary to use Sheikh (chief) (or Sheikha for a woman), Sayed (Mr.), Sayeda (Mrs.), etc. Arabs generally address people by their first names, so John Smith will be addressed as Mr. John. It is important to greet and acknowledge the most senior person in the room first.

When doing business in the Middle East, handshakes are always used and can last a long time. Etiquette recommends that one waits for the other to withdraw their hand first before doing the same. For a man introduced to a woman, it is advisable to wait and see if a hand is extended. Particularly in public, Muslim women are unlikely to shake a man's hand. A Western woman introduced to a Muslim man might also wait to see if he offers his hand. Always use the right hand. Among Muslims, the left hand is reserved for bodily hygiene and considered unclean. The right hand should be used for eating, shaking hands, or handing over an item. Do not be surprised if your hand is held while you are led somewhere. Holding hands among men is common and does not carry the same connotations as it does in the West.

Many people in the Middle East claim a more modest area of personal space than is usual in the West. Accordingly, it can seem rude for an individual to step away when another individual is stepping closer.

Special respect is paid to older people in many circumstances. This can include standing when older people enter a room, always greeting older people first, standing when speaking to one's elders, and serving older people first at a meal.

In terms of gift giving, something personal can be a very meaningful touch. It would be appropriate, although not expected, to present a small or token gift to an individual to whom one is being introduced, say for example a book one has written or very much enjoys, a special company memento, or something related to one's background or hobbies. However, it is not advisable to give a pen or a clock just for the sake of providing a gift. Very senior leaders may or may not provide a gift although it would not be required for one to provide a gift in return.

Gender and attire

Men should avoid touching and prolonged eye contact with Muslim women. It is

---

① Business Etiquette In the Middle East. (2014-05-30) [2022-03-21]. https://businessinmiddleeast.wordpress.com/2014/05/30/business-etiquette-in-the-middle-east/.

considered improper to inquire about a man's wife or daughter. It is polite to ask about family or health, but never specifically about any female members. Family life that involves female members is kept extremely private.

The modesty of one's personal attire is important in the Middle East. Men and women should wear very non-revealing clothes (covering shoulders, arms and legs, and closed-toe shoes) to avoid offending locals. When visiting religious sites, women must also cover their hair. In some circumstances shoes should be removed, such as at the entrance to religious sites.

Business is personal

In the Middle East, doing business revolves much more around personal relationships, family ties, trust and honor. It is therefore important that business relationships be built on mutual friendship and trust. As a consequence of this, if you have friends or contacts in the right places, rules may be bent or things may be done more quickly. The system works on the basis that favors are reciprocated and never forgotten.

Initial meetings are all about relationship-building — building trust and establishing compatibility. One should engage in conversation and try to get to know the person with whom one is doing business.

Age, money, and family connections are all key determining factors of a person's status. Who you are is usually more important than what you have achieved. It is therefore not uncommon to find many members of one family working for the same company.

In conversation, it is always good to ask about the health and well being of a counterpart's family. How many children? (Do not ask how many wives.) What are the children doing? Where have they studied or about to study? Taking interest in a counterpart's family is an important way of building early trust and connection.

Meetings and negotiations

The working week generally is Sunday through Thursday. Punctuality is expected of Westerners — even if it is not practiced by locals. Attitudes to time are more relaxed than in the West, therefore it is not unusual to be kept waiting, though Westerners will be expected to be on time.

Meetings are almost always accompanied by coffee and pastries. Hospitality is held in high regard throughout the Middle East, and people will take great pride in lavish shows of hospitality. To refuse it can cause offense. It is proper etiquette to accept beverages offered and to compliment the host on the food and his hospitality. One should never show the bottom of one's shoes when sitting in a meeting. This is a sign of great disrespect and is a common mistake by Westerners during meetings. As a general rule, displaying the sole of one's foot or touching somebody with one's shoe is considered rude. Meetings can be chaotic. Always be prepared to exercise patience. Cell phone calls, emails or text messages are taken during meetings and people may enter the meeting room unannounced and proceed to discuss their own agenda.

The Arabs, traditionally a trading people, are excellent negotiators and haggling is prevalent from the market to the board room. Decisions are made slowly. Bureaucratic formalities tend to add to delays.

Religion

All of the Gulf countries, including the UAE, Jordan, and Kuwait, are Islamic countries, as is Egypt. Insulting Islam or the prophets is a serious offense. Muslims follow the doctrines of the Koran, which forbids consumption of alcohol, pork products, and shellfish. It is best not to consume these in the presence of government or religious officials. It is also prohibited to drink alcohol in public. Muslims pray five times a day. You will likely hear the calls to prayer, which occur roughly at: between dawn and sunrise, about half an hour after mid-day, mid-afternoon, right after sunset, and an hour and a half after sunset.

Other

People in the Middle East may communicate with a vocal emphasis, volume and body language that others might associate with being angry or upset. Responding to anger or seriousness with light laughter or a smile is common. This must not be seen as a sign that the other person is not taking you or the situation seriously.

UNIT 2

Oil-producing Countries in the Commonwealth of Independent States

Overview

CIS, also referred to as Russian Commonwealth, is a regional organization in Eurasia. The organization was formed after the Soviet Union dissolved. It was formed to encourage cooperation in economic, military and political aspects and it possesses powers to coordinate trade, lawmaking, security and cross-border crime prevention. Currently, the organization consists of 9 member countries, including Armenia, Belarus, Kazakhstan, Kyrgyzstan, Moldova, Russia, Tajikistan, Azerbaijan, and Uzbekistan.①

Task 1 Topic discussion.

List 3 facts you know about CIS countries.

____

____

____

____

____

① GORDON J. Commonwealth of Independent States: Explained. (2021-07-22) [2022-05-09]. https://thebusinessprofessor.com/lesson/commonwealth-of-independent-states-definition/.

Task 2 Listen to the following recording and then fill in the blanks.[①]

Two weeks ago we learned about Andorra, one of the smallest countries on the planet. Today, we will get to know a little about the biggest country in the world, mighty Russia. It measures over 6.5 million square miles, and takes up 1__________ of the Earth's land mass. Because it is so huge, its coastline borders on 15 seas, two of which are the Pacific and the Arctic oceans. It shares some of its borders with 13 other countries. There are about 2__________ people living there, mainly in European Russia, which is the part of the country that is closest to Europe. There you can find a 3__________ of cities such as the capital, Moscow, St. Petersburg, Stalingrad, and also those of southwestern Siberia.

The climate in Russia is difficult to summarize. Because there are vast areas of land which are far from the sea, these areas have extremely cold winters and extremely hot summers, with spring and autumn being short. The coastal areas are more regulated by the 4__________. Siberia, to the north, has an obvious 5__________ influence, and has only one month of summer in the far north. However, in its sunny southern area, there is a very large population, and successful farming.

It is difficult to sum up history of such an enormous and ancient country as Russia in a simple paragraph, so I will just hit upon some of the major historical points. Russia, up until the 6th century, was 6__________ by nomadic tribes. Peoples from Iran and Turkey settled in the south, but were overrun by Vikings who established power. In the 10th century, the Russian leader Vladimir was 7__________ to Christianity. For two hundred years, the Russian Orthodox Church thrived, until the Mongols took over. They were 8__________ in the 15th century and the first Tsar, "Ivan the Terrible" declared himself supreme ruler. The last of the Tsars, Nicholas the second abdicated and was assassinated in 1917, giving way to the Communist Party under Lenin. Russia then endured a civil war, huge losses in the Second World War, and then the Cold War. The Soviet Union was officially 9__________ in 1991, and formed a Commonwealth of Independent States. Russia has the largest reserves of natural gas in the world, and is very rich in 10__________. Wealth is bringing transforming power, and infrastructural and social changes are being experienced as a result. This vast and rapidly changing country is closely watched by the rest of the world because of its "super" status, influence, and modernization.

① The audio can be accessed here: https://www.tingclass.net/show-8729-265142-1.html.

Task 3 Watch the video about Kazakhstan and answer the questions.①

1. What is the location, size and population of Kazakhstan?

____

____

2. What are the three biggest cities of Kazakhstan?

____

____

3. What is the role of horse in Kazakhstan?

____

____

4. What is the unique culture of Kazakhstan?

____

____

Task 4 Watch the following videos about Maslenitsa and answer the questions.②

Brief introduction to Maslenitsa: Maslenitsa, also known as Butter Week, Crepe week, or Cheesefare Week, is an Eastern Slavic religious and folk holiday, celebrated during the last week before Great Lent, that is, the eighth week before Eastern Orthodox Pascha (Easter).

1. Why do they celebrate Maslenitsa?

____

____

2. What are the traditions of Maslenitsa?

____

____

① The video can be accessed here: https://www.bilibili.com/video/BV1wz411v7p9/?spm_id_from=333.788.recommend_more_video.7&vd_source=8bb6197478437eca7f140934e62b43c9.

② The videos can be accessed here: https://news.cgtn.com/news/2021-03-15/Russians-burn-24-meter-castle-symbolizing-COVID-19-at-Maslenitsa-YEBIb8rrwc/index.html; https://news.cgtn.com/news/3d45444e78636a4d/index.html?t=1488115416519.recommend_more_video.7&vd_source=8bb6197478437eca7f140934e62b43c9.

Task 5 Understand Russia through TV series.

Serial *How I became Russian* was filmed in Moscow Russia 2015. It tells about the experience of an American journalist, Alex Wilson, who is sent by his employer, *The American Post*, one of the largest newspapers in the world, on a long-term assignment in their Moscow office. In addition to his job there as an editor, Alex starts a blog, where he tries to answer important questions about Russians, Russian culture, and the mythical and elusive Russian soul.

Watch the first six episodes of the series and try to answer the following questions.

1. What did Alex think of Russia before he went there?

____

____

2. What does "smile" mean in Russia?

____

____

3. Why is Alex's boss angry when she receives his flowers?

____

____

4. What problem does Alex have when he looks for a plumber?

____

____

5. In what ways are Russians superstitious?

____

____

Lead in

Do some research and find out information about the major oil-producing countries in CIS. Finish the following table:

Rank	Country	Production	Top oil and gas companies
1			
2			
3			
4			

Text A

The Great Silk Road in Kazakhstan[①]

For centuries, crowds of people speaking diverse languages filled the bazaars of Asia, and long caravans crept along dusty roads carrying precious gems and silks, spices and dyes, gold and silver, and exotic birds and animals to Europe.

Yet the Silk Road was to become not only a great trade route but the melting pot of two very different civilizations: those of the East and the West, with their specific cultural traditions, religious beliefs, and scientific and technical achievements. Central Asia, situated between China and India in the east, bordering on the European world in the west, spreading between the Volga and Siberia in the north, and between Persia and Arabia in the south, for almost two thousand years stood at the crossroads of the world's great civilizations and cultures.

Much has been lost to history. The sands of time have covered many ancient towns, but the careful hands of archeologists and restorers have succeeded in finding and restoring for us rare treasures from the old cultures of the Semirechye (Seven Rivers region) and Central Asia.

Branches and routes of the Silk Route didn't remain static over the course of time — they changed for various reasons: Some of them gained significance and flourished, while others ceased to exist, causing the decline of the towns and settlements in their paths.

In the sixth and seventh centuries A.D. the route passed through China to the west via the Semirechye and southern Kazakhstan. The flourishing period of the Silk Road through Central

① Kazakhstan Section of the Silk Road. [2022-05-03]. https://www.orexca.com/kazakhstan/silk_road.htm.

Asia and Kazakhstan declined during the 8th–12th centuries.

The huge territory remembers the slow plodding of camel caravans, for thousands of years wandering the wide routes of the Great Silk Road.

This part of the road represents a unique complex of historical monuments, archeology, architecture, town planning and monumental art. The cities of Otrar, Taraz, Turkestan, Sairam (Ispidzhab), Suyab, Balasagun and others were not only shopping centers, but centers of science and culture.

Taraz

In ancient times the town was called the "town of merchants". Narrow streets, like streams, ran towards the center — the noisy bazaar. The bazaar of Taraz was the focus of the city's life. It was thanks to the bazaar that the town came into being, with a citadel, mosques, caravanserais, mud-walled cottages, walled courtyards and craftsmen's workshops. It seemed that people from all over the world were coming to the bazaar in order to sell, buy or exchange something. One could sell and buy practically anything. The ancients were right to say: "Taraz bazaar is the mirror of the world."

Over the course of many centuries it was a center of non-ferrous metallurgy. The copper articles of Taraz workshops such as jugs, cosmetic boxes, lamps, decorations for armaments, clothes and harnesses traveled all over the world. An example of casting art is the ritual teapot (Kazakh) in the mausoleum of Ahmet Yasavi in Turkestan; it is second to none in its dimensions. Its diameter is 2.2 m, and weight 2 tons.

In 1896, at the All-Russia exhibition in Nizhny Novgorod, Kazakh bracelets made of silver caused a real sensation, and they were awarded gold medals.

The present-day green bazaar is on the very spot of the ancient bazaar of two thousand years ago. When you walk along its rows, you feel the dust of millennia under your feet.

Otrar

"Traveler! Here are the ruins of the fortress town that stemmed for half a year the advance of the Mongol hordes to Central Asia and the Caucasus, Russia and the Eastern European countries, and which showed resistance to foreign invaders in the following centuries", runs the inscription on the cast-iron plate installed on the entrance to the Otrar archeological reserve and museum. The Otrar oasis included over 150 small towns, fortresses, castles and fortified settlements, connected to one another by a chain of caravanserais of the Great Silk Road. In its heyday, the population of Otrar numbered about a quarter of a million.

The first permanent settlement in the Otrar area is dated to the 2nd century B.C. Its founders were the Kangyus — descendants of the Saks.

Otrar is the birthplace of the great scientist and philosopher of the Middle Ages, Abu

Nasra ibn Mohammed who entered history under the name of Al Farabi. The thinker lived between the years 870 and 950. Thanks to his philosophical thinking and encyclopedic knowledge, he was called the second teacher of mankind, after Aristotle, when he was still alive. His treatise on the classification of sciences opened a way for scholarship in the centuries ahead. It is natural that all the great scientists after him, such as Avicenna, Al-Biruni, Shirazee, Makhmud Kashgari, Yusuf Ballasafuni, Ulugbek, and ibn al-Farabi considered themselves to be his disciples.

Turkestan

Another ancient town on the Great Silk Road was Turkestan, which is 1,500 years old. The town came into being in 490 A.D. The town of Yasa saw its greatest prosperity in the 7th century. At that time it was a motley, crowded maze with its abundant bazaars and endless caravans. The fame of the town spread all across the Islamic world. To a certain extent, this was due to the name of Hodja Ahmed ibn Ibragim al Yasawi, a dervish and advocate of Sufism, and the founder of the ascetic brotherhood of Yasavia which translated verses into the language of ordinary people. His poems became very popular; his ardent sermons attracted a large number of pilgrims. It was at that time that Yasa was called "a second Mecca".

Sufism is a religious teaching that combines orthodox Islam and popular beliefs. In his private life and with the help of simple easily understood language, Hodja Ahmed Yasavi called upon people to be kind, meek, and obedient and not to be greedy. Ahmed Yasavi's fame did not dwindle after his death. Thousands of pilgrims thronged to his grave. The first mausoleum built over the sheikh's grave was very modest and became dilapidated as the years passed. A new mausoleum was erected 233 years after his death on Tamerlane's orders. At present, Ahmed Yasavi's mausoleum has been restored to its original appearance. The town is becoming a major center of world tourism.

Sairam (Ispidzhab)

In the time of the caravan trade existed another very important ancient town — Ispidzhab or Sairam. In the historical chronicles of the 9th and 10th centuries, Ispidzhab was called a first class military fortress. The Arabs named this town one of the best in the East for its independence and dignity, attaching the name "white town" to it.

Many disasters befell Ispidzhab after some devastating wars. There is nothing left of the fine gardens and fortifications but ruined walls, and rotten and broken trees. In the 15th century the town was restored to life under the name of Sairam, and once more it was surrounded by strong fortified walls and trenches.

After its subsequent destruction in 1684, Sairam was not able to recover its former name. Currently, there are very few remains of the past fame of white town, such as the ruins of walls and bastions, the minaret of the demolished Bazalakata (12th century), a mosque with a spiral staircase and the half-destroyed entrance to a basement leading no one knows where.

Some religious structures remind you of the past of Sairam, such as the two monuments connected with the name of Hodja Ahmjet Yasavi, which were built after the Dzungar invasion. His parents were buried in Ispidzhab. After the erection of the tomb to Hodja Ahmet Yasavi in Sairam, monuments were erected to his parents — Ibraghim ata and Karachach ana.

Suyab and Balasagun

Suyab was the first capital of the western Turkic Kaganat, which was formed in 581 as a busy trade center. Every year merchants from different countries came to a big fair where they sold and bought goods and discussed commercial matters.

Suyab was the ancient capital of the Semirechye Turks, the forefathers of the Kazakh ethnic group, and Balasagun was the first town where the Turks were first introduced to the Koran. The towns were re-ordered many times but it was rather difficult to determine their exact geopolitical positions.

For about two thousand years, caravans drove along the Great Silk Road. Nothing could stop their measured steps. The world was shaken by bloody wars and devastating epidemics. Peoples and states sprang to life and then suddenly disappeared. Even the Amu Darya changed its course and sources; the Aral Sea changed its outline and only three Silk Road cities remained unchanged.

Exercises

Task 1 Complete the following sentences based on text A.

1. The ________ of Taraz was the focus of the city's life in ancient times.
2. Otrar was a ________ town and resisted the foreign invaders. It was also birthplace of ________.
3. Turkestan is ________ years old. Its name spread to the ________ world to some extent because of Hodja Ahmed ibn Ibragim al Yasawi.
4. Sairam was called a ________ military fortress. The Arabs named it ________ for its independence and dignity.
5. Suyab was the first ________ of the western Turkic Kaganat, which was formed in 581 as a busy ________.

Task 2 Answer the following questions according to the information from text A.

1. How did branches and routes of the Silk Route change over the course of time?

____

____

2. How do you understand "Taraz bazaar is the mirror of the world"?

____

____

3. Why was Yasa called "a second Mecca" in the 7th century?

____

____

4. What is Sairam like currently?

____

____

5. Which of the cities listed in the text still exist?

____

____

Task 3 Translate the following sentences into Chinese.

1. Yet the Silk Road was to become not only a great trade route but the melting pot of two very different civilizations; those of the East and the West, with their specific cultural traditions, religious beliefs, and scientific and technical achievements.

____

____

2. Here are the ruins of the fortress town that stemmed for half a year the advance of the Mongol hordes to Central Asia and the Caucasus, Russia and the Eastern European countries, and which showed resistance to foreign invaders in the following centuries.

____

____

3. Currently, there are very few remains of the past fame of white town, such as the ruins of walls and bastions, the minaret of the demolished Bazalakata (12th century), a mosque with a spiral staircase and the half-destroyed entrance to a basement leading no one knows where.

____

____

Task 4 Critical thinking enhancement.

With 10 years of progress, the Belt and Road Initiative (BRI) has transitioned from a blueprint for shared development to concrete infrastructure projects and business contracts, and it is being raised to a higher level. Kazakhstan is an active participant of the BRI. What achievements have been made between Kazakhstan and China under the framework of the BRI?

____

____

____

____

____

Text B

Orthodox Churches in Russia①

Church of the Saviour on Spilled Blood

The Church of the Saviour on Spilled Blood is one of St. Petersburg's most impressive churches. With multicolored onion domes reminiscent of St. Basil's Cathedral in Moscow, the Church of the Saviour on Spilled Blood is a breathtaking sight both outside and within its ornately decorated walls.

Whilst this church is also known as the Church on Spilt Blood, its official name is the Church of the Resurrection of Jesus Christ. In fact the construction of the Church of the Saviour on Spilled Blood originally began in 1883 by Emperor Alexander Ⅲ to commemorate his father, Alexander Ⅱ. Alexander Ⅱ was actually assassinated on the site where the church was built in 1881, thus lending the Russian Orthodox cathedral its alternative name referring to spilled blood.

Completed in 1907 during the reign of Nicholas Ⅱ, the Church of the Saviour on Spilled Blood is an incredible mixture of colours and design. Unlike most of the buildings in St. Petersburg, it is not built in a Baroque or neoclassical style, but rather a more medieval Russian one. Inside, the Church of the Saviour on Spilled Blood is densely adorned with 7,000 square metres of vivid mosaics created by world famous Russian artists such as Mikhail Vrubel and Viktor Vasnetsov.

The Church of the Saviour on Spilled Blood has had a varied history, from its original consecration and veneration to being looted and damaged in the aftermath of the Russian Revolution and being used as a storage facility for the deceased during the Second World War and as a potato storage facility afterwards. It was only in the 1970s that the church was reopened and in 1997, after 27 years of renovation, that it was returned to its former glory.

The Cathedral of Christ the Saviour

Although the Cathedral now stands out in the Moscow skyline, with its gold cupola

---

① ROLLER S. Church of the Saviour on Spilled Blood. (2020-11-24) [2022-05-09]. https://www.historyhit.com/locations/church-of-the-saviour-on-spilled-blood/.
Cathedral of Christ the Saviour, Moscow. [2022-05-09]. https://www.expresstorussia.com/guide/moscow_cathedral_of_christ.html.
SULLIVAN A I. St. Basil's Cathedral: Medieval Russia's Iconic Building. (2021-05-29) [2022-09-09]. https://www.medievalists.net/2021/05/st-basils-cathedral-medieval-russias-iconic-building/.

shining over the city, the Cathedral has only recently been reconstructed. The history of the Cathedral begins on December 25, 1812. This was the day that the last soldiers of Napoleons' 600,000-man army were driven out of Russia. Emperor Alexander Ⅰ signed a Manifesto ordering the construction of a magnificent Cathedral in honour of Christ the Saviour in Moscow as a thanksgiving to God and to honour the victorious Russian army.

The first site was on the Sparrow Hills. However, unsteady ground and underground waters made this site unfeasible. On April 10, 1832 Emperor Nicholas Ⅰ approved a new project — on the bank of the Moscow River, near the Kremlin. The cornerstone was laid on September 10, 1839.

The Cathedral took forty years to build and of course, only the best architects, builders and artists of the time fulfilled the designs. Overall, the Cathedral is modelled on ancient Russian churches built in the Byzantine style. However, it differs from Byzantine archetypes with its more regular shape and lighter form.

The Great Consecration of the Cathedral took place on Ascension, on May 26, 1883, which was also the day Alexander Ⅲ was crowned. Regular services were conducted in the Cathedral from this time on. All important church and civic events were marked in the Cathedral.

After the revolution, the site of the Cathedral, along with ideological principles, became the reason for the decision to destroy the Cathedral. The plan entailed constructing a grandiose Palace of Soviets on the site of the Cathedral. In 1931 it was destroyed. The planned palace was never built. During the thaw, the city built an enormous swimming pool instead of the Cathedral.

In 1990, The Holy Synod of the Russian Orthodox Church blessed the reconstruction of the Cathedral of Christ the Saviour. The Synod appealed to the Russian government asking for permission to resurrect the Cathedral on its original site. The reconstruction of the Cathedral began in 1994. Although the Cathedral wasn't officially consecrated until 2000, it was used for services, festivals and other important events during its restoration.

Saint Basil's Cathedral

St. Basil's Cathedral was a commemorative monument to the victories of Ivan Ⅳ in the Russo-Kazan Wars of 1552. These events significantly expanded the borders of Ivan Ⅳ's domain, helping transform the Russian State into an empire with far-reaching control. The territorial and economic growth under Ivan Ⅳ also enabled the Russian tsar to turn his attention toward building projects, like the impressive new structure of St. Basil's Cathedral.

The new cathedral was built using mainly red brick on a foundation of white stone. The complex consists of nine main chapels or "tower-churches" organized in a symmetrical pattern and offering a staggered ascending impression from the exterior. Onion domes, a hallmark of

Russian architecture, cap the tops of these tall chapels. With no parallel in Byzantine or Slavic religious building, St. Basil's Cathedral is intriguing from an architectural standpoint and in terms of its dazzling design and colorful decorative features.

A 156-foot high central nave and a massive multifaceted central tower on the exterior define the core of the church. From the exterior, thus, St. Basil's Cathedral offers the impression of an ascending, layered, and "flame-like" structure focused on the central massive tower. Originally, St. Basil's Cathedral's appearance was mainly white with golden cupolas crowning each of the towers. After the 1583 fire that greatly damaged the building, the golden domes of the tower cupolas were replaced with the onion domes. These now-famous domes received their multi-colored appearance in 1670. The rich and vibrant colors for which the building is celebrated today also date to these seventeenth-century restoration projects.

Although the mastermind behind the design of St. Basil's Cathedral remains unknown, some scholars have proposed an architect of Italian origin. The Russian chronicles also name two local architects, although they could be one and the same person: Barma and Postnik Yakovlev (Postnik could be a nickname for Barma). Nevertheless, the actual process through which the designer(s) arrived at the eclectic visual appearance of St. Basil's Cathedral with features and forms drawn from distinct building traditions remains elusive.

Legend also has it that supposedly Ivan Ⅳ blinded St. Basil's Cathedral's architect(s) so that the designs of his new and impressive structure could not be replicated in any other subsequent building. Although such accounts cannot be verified, they do align with what is known of Ivan Ⅳ's complex personality and aspects of his severe and capricious temperament. Sources note episodes of mental outbreaks, with one notable tragic instance, detailed in visual and textual sources, in which Ivan Ⅳ killed his own son during an argument. Other accounts speak of his harsh treatment of Russian nobility.

Until the completion of the renovations on Ivan the Great's Bell Tower in the Kremlin in 1600, St. Basil's Cathedral stood as the tallest building in Moscow. As a symbol of Moscow and one of the city's most famous tourist attractions today, St. Basil's Cathedral remains a prominent centerpiece of the Red Square. It is designated as a UNESCO World Heritage site, and today serves as a museum.

Exercises

Task 1 Match the churches with the relevant information.

1. Church of the Saviour on Spilled Blood ____________________

2. The Cathedral of Christ the Saviour ____________________

3. Saint Basil's Cathedral ______________________________

a. It was built to honor the Tsar who was assassinated on the site.
b. Its construction was ordered by the Tsar to mark the victory of Russia in the Russo-Kazan Wars.
c. It was destroyed during Soviet Union period and was reconstructed in the 1990s.
d. It was damaged during the Russian Revolution and was once used to store things.
e. It was originally all white but now it is in many colors.
f. It was built to thank the God for helping the Russian army drive Napoleon's army out of Russia.
g. Legend says that the builders were made blind after it was built.

Task 2 Use the proper forms of the words in the table to complete the following sentences. You may not use any of the words in the table more than once.

ornately	commemorate	adorn	renovation	entail
enormous	resurrect	symmetrical	intriguing	replicate

1. Curtained alcoves and spacious main seating areas are ________ furnished with Chinese antiques and lanterns.
2. The couple spent thousands ________ the house.
3. Attempts to ________ the ceasefire have already failed once.
4. One room contained a gallery of paintings ________ great moments in baseball history.
5. His watercolour designs ________ a wide range of books.
6. Cells can reproduce but only molecules can ________.
7. Such a decision would ________ a huge political risk.
8. The ________ design of this church makes it very beautiful.
9. It is an ________ challenge but we hope to meet it within a year or 18 months.
10. This ________ book is both thoughtful and informative.

Task 3 Translate the following sentences into Chinese.

1. The Church of the Saviour on Spilled Blood has had a varied history, from its original consecration and veneration to being looted and damaged in the aftermath of the Russian Revolution and being used as a storage facility for the deceased during the Second World War and as a potato storage facility afterwards.

____

____

2. Emperor Alexander Ⅰ signed a Manifesto ordering the construction of a magnificent Cathedral in honour of Christ the Saviour in Moscow as a thanksgiving to God and to honour the victorious Russian army.

____

____

3. Nevertheless, the actual process through which the designer(s) arrived at the eclectic visual appearance of St. Basil's Cathedral with features and forms drawn from distinct building traditions remains elusive.

____

____

Task 4 Please write an essay of 300 words to discuss the following issue.

People-to-people and cultural exchanges have been an integral part of China–Russian relations. Can you give any suggestions on how to enhance the mutual understanding and friendship between Chinese and Russian people, especially between the youth?

____

____

____

____

____

Text C

Intangible Cultural Heritage of Azerbaijan

Azerbaijani culture dates back to centuries ago. Numerous pearls of Azerbaijani culture and architecture have been inscribed in the UNESCO World Heritage List and Intangible Cultural Heritage List. This text introduces two representatives which are listed as Intangible Cultural Heritage in Need of Urgent Safeguarding.

National spirit: the Azerbaijani sport that makes horse sense①

It's the Azerbaijani national sport, recognized for its rich cultural significance and inextricably linked with the country's favorite animal, but playing it is not for the faint-hearted. Welcome to Chovgan, a forerunner of polo. Its roots can be traced back to the middle of the first millennium, and it doesn't have any frills.

Although the basic rules are pretty much the same as those of polo, there are no helmets or safety gear for players. Chovgan is a game of skill but, more than anything else, it is one of courage.

• Karabakh stallions

Players ride Karabakh stallions, mountain steppe racing and riding horses noted for their speed and stamina and unique to Azerbaijan, often without saddles. Pickup games between village teams remain common, with working farm horses taking a break from their labors to do a little sporting duty. But the key trait of Chovgan, those who know and play it say, is the sort of attitude and bravery that are needed to shine.

"People who are a little bit afraid of some action in life cannot do this," Bahruz Nabiyev, the head of Azerbaijan's Equestrian Federation, says.

• A long history

Nabiyev explains just how deeply the sport is embedded in the life of the country. "This is part of the history of Azerbaijan," he adds. "Every Azerbaijani person has a kind of love for the horses because of the history. It was a hobby for the people. Actually, shepherds were playing this game many years ago, and then they started to make it as a game in Azerbaijan, and make a championship of it."

Both Chovgan and the Karabakh horse are officially recognized by world heritage body

① BORG C, NEWTON P, MORTENSEN A. National Spirit: The Azerbaijani Sport That Makes Horse Sense. (2015-06-12) [2022-09-21]. https://edition.cnn.com/2015/06/10/sport/azerbaijan-chovgan-karabakh-horses-polo/index.html.

UNESCO, and Nabiyev and his colleagues hope the expertise of the country's best players can enable them to make a mark on international polo.

- A protected species

It also appears that the battle to safeguard the future of the Karabakh horse is being won after years in which growing alarm was voiced about dwindling numbers. Yashar Guluzade, who has been breeding the animals in the forested foothills of Sheki, a small city 300 km (187 miles) from the capital, Baku, explains that conflict and a difficult economic situation led to a decline.

"At the beginning of the Armenian-Azerbaijani conflict [in the late 1980s] the horses were continually transferred from one place to another, and this was one of the reasons for the sharp reduction of stock as the movement of pregnant mares led to miscarriages," he told CNN.

The government has stepped in to try and protect the breed, with the Ministry of Agriculture drawing up a number of horse breeding programs and introducing a law prohibiting the export of Karabakh horses for sale.

Estimates of the number of Karabakh horses — named after the mountain region where they were originally developed through cross-breeding — vary. According to the Karabakh Foundation, there were fewer than 1,000 in 2011. The foundation's co-founder Dr. Adil Baguirov, originally from the Karabakh region, says the horse has always been important to Azerbaijanis. As Khandan Rajabli, the head of the Ministry of Agriculture's breeding division, puts it: "The Karabakh horses are a symbol of national heritage and pride. It's an ancient, national breed that is inseparable from our national identity."

Yalli: a masterpiece of Azerbaijani folk dance①

Yalli, a traditional group dance, is considered the pearl and the oldest type of Azerbaijani culture.

These dances are an expression of the past, present and national traditions of the Azerbaijani people. It takes a great effort to preserve this folkloric heritage called a symbol of antiquity, which is transmitted from generation to generation through the centuries to the present day.

One can hardly imagine a significant celebration in the country without these graceful movements, performed for hundreds of years at festivals and folk games, weddings and entertaining simulations of battles.

---

① BILLUPS M M. Yalli — A Masterpiece of Azerbaijani Folk Dance, Safeguarded by UNESCO as Intangible Cultural Heritage. (2022-01-24)[2022-09-21]. https://dorndancecompany.com/yalli-a-masterpiece-of-azerbaijani-folk-dance-safeguarded-by-unesco-as-intangible-cultural-heritage-azertac/.

The history of dance art in Azerbaijan dates back to the Stone Age. A clear proof of this fact are petroglyphs resembling the Azerbaijani yalli round dance, which meet visitors at the entrance to the Gobustan State Historical and Art Reserve, a UNESCO World Heritage Site. The heritage site is full of images of people dancing among the many petroglyphs. Some of these images show people dancing while holding hands as if performing yalli. These millennial images once again confirm the fact that the yalli dance appeared on this land a very long time ago.

Experts have estimated that there are more than a thousand varieties of yalli in Azerbaijan, including "Kochari" "Uchayag" "Tello" "Tenzere" and "Galadangalaya". Remarkably, a hundred of these dances are cherished in Nakhichevan, an ancient land of Azerbaijan.

The common feature of all types is that it is performed as a cheerful circular dance often accompanied by choral singing. The dancers hold each other's hands or shoulders and perform synchronous rhythmic movements, raising and lowering their arms, while the pace and rhythm of the steps are determined by the main dancer.

Typically, yalli dances involve elements of games, pantomime (imitations of birds or other animals), physical exercises, and movement.

Joyful sounds of yalli can also be heard in Azerbaijani villages during holidays, especially in Novruz, which is one of the most important favorite holidays of Azerbaijanis solemnly celebrated both at home and abroad.

Yalli tunes, widely known and popular in the country, were also used by prominent Azerbaijani composer Uzeyir Hajibayli in the opera "Korogly", legendary opera and music performer Muslim Magomayev in the opera "Nargiz", as well as the famous composer and conductor Soltan Hajibayov in the ballet "Gulshan".

One of the best showcases of Azerbaijani yalli dancing took place during the opening ceremony of the first European Games when President Ilham Aliyev declared the Games open following a spectacular celebration held in the capital Baku in June 2015.

As the fireworks grew in intensity, all of the performers gathered around the edge of the circular stage. They held hands and danced the yalli, the national dance of Azerbaijan. During the yalli, the names of all of the Ceremony's volunteer performers appeared on the LED strip that ran along a balcony of the stadium, scrolling along its entire length. Twenty thousand inflatable "pomegranate seeds" swept over the audience. They were a token of love and good luck and a symbol of Azerbaijan. This joyous yalli dance ended the opening ceremony.

Traditional yalli (Kochari, Tenzere) group dances of Nakhichevan were inscribed on UNESCO's list of Intangible Cultural Heritage in Need of Urgent Safeguarding during the 13th session of UNESCO's Intergovernmental Committee for the Safeguarding of Intangible

Cultural Heritage which was held in Port Louis, Republic of Mauritius in 2018. The nomination documents were jointly submitted by the Azerbaijani Ministry of Culture, the Ministry of Foreign Affairs and the Permanent Mission of Azerbaijan to UNESCO.

Exercises

Task 1 Answer the following questions according to the information from text C.

1. How do you understand "Chovgan is a game of skill but, more than anything else, it is one of courage"?

____

____

2. What measures does Azerbaijani government take to protect Karabakh horses?

____

____

3. How is yalli performed?

____

____

Task 2 Translate the following sentences into Chinese.

1. It's the Azerbaijani national sport, recognized for its rich cultural significance and inextricably linked with the country's favorite animal, but playing it is not for the faint-hearted.

____

____

2. These dances are an expression of the past, present and national traditions of the Azerbaijani people. It takes a great effort to preserve this folkloric heritage called a symbol of antiquity, which is transmitted from generation to generation through the centuries to the present day.

____

____

3. One of the best showcases of Azerbaijani yalli dancing took place during the opening ceremony of the first European Games when President Ilham Aliyev declared the Games open following a spectacular celebration held in the capital Baku in June 2015.

____

____

Task 3 Expanded learning.

Choose another element from the lists of Intangible Cultural Heritage in Azerbaijan (https://ich.unesco.org/en/state/azerbaijan-AZ?info=elements-on-the-lists) and prepare a presentation about it.

____

____

____

____

____

Practical Tips

Russia: Business Practices[①]

The fundamental principles of business culture

Russian business culture has undergone a tremendous change since dissolution of the Soviet Union; however, traditional standards and values still linger. Russian professionals are known as tough negotiators. While honest in their approach, Russians can also be pretty unforgiving. Despite the ongoing transformation and generational differences, business culture is characterised by the following traits: caution, persistence and modesty. Patience and perseverance are also key to closing a deal.

The Soviet mentality persists in most firms regarding their managerial approach. Decisions are made from the top down and subordinates rarely take initiative or "deviate" from the position of their company. In fact, most Russian professionals speak with one voice, reaffirming a single position. Decision-making usually takes long time and is sometimes extended on purpose to test the foreign side's willingness to compromise. Nevertheless, once a decision is made, the Russian side may also want to sign a deal very quickly and engage in business almost immediately.

Personal relationships are key to signing a good deal with Russian professionals. Close ties are built on the basis of trust and honesty, and can sometimes be the only motivator that helps achieve progress during deadlocks in negotiations. Relationship building usually takes time as Russians would want to believe you are authentic and understand your personal goals and ambitions rather than your personal objectives. Business entertaining (drinking in particular) is a fast and efficient way to build relationships.

First contact

It is difficult to do business in Russia without the help of a local connection. Older people may also be more suspicious of foreigners and people they do not know whereas the younger generation is getting used to engaging in business with foreign associates. Appointments should be made well in advance and reconfirmed several days prior to the actual date of meeting. It should not come too much as a surprise if they are cancelled on short notice. Russians are often not very proficient in English, and it is safer to check with your Russian counterparts whether

---

① Russia: Business Practice. [2022-05-15]. https://www.scbtrade.com/en/portal/explore-new-markets/country-profiles/russia/business-practices.

an interpreter will be necessary.

Time management

Punctuality is highly regarded in Russia and foreigners are always expected to arrive on time. Nevertheless, Russian professionals may not always be on time and can even be late just to test the patience of their foreign counterparts. Meetings do not always have a set agenda and senior Russian executives may determine the course of the meeting. Meetings are most likely to run over time and be followed by a lunch or dinner that will allow Russian associates to get to know their foreign counterparts.

Greetings and titles

When meeting someone, a light handshake is appropriate. Handshakes are on the firm side and it is important to maintain eye contact while shaking hands. A slight nod of acknowledgment may also suffice.

Gift policy

Exchanging gifts during an initial meeting is common in Russia. Small gifts with your company logo or representative of your country are appropriate for the first meeting. If invited to a Russian home, it is always a good idea to bring gifts, ideally flowers, fine chocolate/sweets or wine/liquor.

Dress code

The dress code is formal both for men and women. Russians value being well dressed and nicely groomed. Men are expected to wear dark coloured suits with shirt and tie, and stylish and conservative business suits, and dresses or trousers are appropriate for women. Business casual or an informal attire are not considered appropriate.

Business cards

Business cards are widely exchanged in Russia. While there is no specific protocol surrounding the exchange of cards, it is recommended to have one side of the business card translated into Russian. Putting any advanced degrees on the business card is also a good idea as they are likely to impress Russian associates.

Meetings management

The first meeting usually serves the purpose of establishing credibility and determining if a relationship is worth forging. Meetings, especially the first ones, are likely to have a formal atmosphere and follow a very strict procedure. Russian professionals may ask to sign off on a "protokol" at the end of a meeting, which is similar to minutes.

When introducing an offer, it is important to provide a long and detailed presentation that refers to precedent cases on the subject. As Russians are generally less flexible and adaptable, new ideas should be introduced gently and directions as personal recommendations rather than official requirements. These ideas may also cause discomfort and put Russian professionals in an awkward position, as they cannot commit before they have sought approval from higher up. On the other hand, flexibility and willingness to compromise can be seen as a sign of weakness. If negotiations come to a deadlock, Russians usually prefer to patiently wait it out unless the other side is especially firm in their position. This is a tactic to push foreign counterparts to grant more concessions out of impatience. Despite their willingness to engage in business, Russians may also walk away from the deal and cancel meetings at last minute to test the flexibility of their foreign counterparts.

During meetings, it is important to talk to Russian counterparts as equals and not to come across as condescending. As Russians are usually quite status-conscious, it is recommended to ensure your team matches the Russian team in terms of number and rank. This status consciousness also makes procedural details such as seating arrangements and speaking orders quite important. It is recommended not to single out a Russian from the group to speak out, as this may be considered as a form of dissidence. Russians tend to display emotions in meetings and negotiations may include heightened tempers. Some Russian professionals may even storm out of the meeting room; therefore, it is important to hold your ground. Interruptions during meetings are common as participants follow different discussions. It is recommended to maintain direct eye contact while speaking and not to show the soles of your shoes as this is considered rude.

Business entertaining is an important part of the working culture, especially drinking and toasting. An invitation to go out for a drink shows a sign of interest in strengthening the relationship. Business dinners at the home of the Russian associate are also quite common. When invited for a business entertaining event, it is very important to follow the host (i.e. when to start eating, when to get up, when to start talking about business).

Things You Should Never, Ever Do in Azerbaijan①

Azerbaijan mixes elements of Persian, Turkish and Russian culture with deep local traditions. Tourists should try their best to avoid doing something unintentionally that might

① BEDFORD S. 11 Things You Should Never, Ever Do in Azerbaijan. (2018-01-31) [2022-05-16]. https://theculturetrip.com/europe/azerbaijan/articles/11-things-never-ever-azerbaijan/.

cause offence or cause themselves problems. Here are a few seemingly innocuous things a foreigner should avoid doing in Azerbaijan culture at all costs.

Don't forget to register with the State Migration Service

Foreigners who plan to spend longer than 10 days in Azerbaijan need to register their presence with the State Migration Service. Hotels and hostels usually register on behalf of guests while those staying in Airbnb have to do it themselves. As of 2018, it's possible to do this online. Failure to do so leads to a hefty fine when leaving the country.

Don't litter

Walk through the streets of Baku and notice the cleanliness. Rubbish bins line the streets, and people use them. Not only does littering come with a hefty fine, but it's considered a little taboo in Azerbaijani culture. Litter will be more visible in rural areas and near local markets but the capital itself tends to be clean.

Don't say negative things about Azerbaijan to locals

When Azerbaijanis give some of the best hospitality in the world, the last thing they want is to listen to tourists complaining. Locals know the pitfalls of their country. They don't need arrogant tourists pointing it out. After all, Azerbaijan has lots of beautiful places and a vibrant culture behind the negative views in the media.

Don't be rude to women

Being rude in Azerbaijan culture might have a different meaning compared to back at home. Men respect women and Azerbaijanis expect foreigners to do the same. Women always have priority in public transport and males stand up to give their seats. If an Azerbaijani woman is invited out, the man pays.

Don't take a taxi from the airport

Unless the wallet oozes with cash or there's a credit card on the business account, avoid using the airport taxis. Walk out Heydar Aliyev International Airport and see a swarm of London-style black cabs trying to entice tourists with inflated prices to Baku. The Airport Express Bus runs every 30 minutes to Baku's central transport hub at 28 May Metro Station. The journey doesn't take much longer, and bus tickets cost approximately 5% of a taxi.

Don't rely on tours for everything

Another point millionaires can ignore. The recent surge of visitors from the Middle East has caused the cost of tours to skyrocket. Often a day trip costs at least $70 per person with a driver. Adventurous tourists using public transport spend as little as $5 to get there and back.

Don't forget to bring your passport when you go out

According to the law, foreigners need to carry their passports at all times. Police occasionally stop and check the identity of tourists. Anyone who doesn't have their documents might face a fine. A photocopy is usually enough, but it's best to double check.

Don't accept gifts straightaway

If someone offers a gift, it's polite to refuse twice and accept on the third time. The same will be true when someone gives a gift to an Azerbaijani. Stay respectful, express gratitude and make a big deal of hoping it didn't cause them an inconvenience.

Don't make the OK sign

In the West, touching the forefinger against the thumb to make a circle symbolises everything is okay. Not in Azerbaijan culture. The sign is considered to be rude and offensive just like in Turkey. While we're on the subject, pointing with the finger is a big no-no too. Instead, use the entire hand to gesture in the general direction.

UNIT 3

Oil-producing Countries in Africa

Overview

The culture of Africa is varied and manifold, consisting of a mixture of countries with various tribes that have their own unique characteristic from the continent of Africa. It is a product of the diverse populations that today inhabit the continent of Africa and the African Diaspora. African culture is expressed in its arts and crafts, folklore and religion, clothing, cuisine, music and languages. Expressions of culture are abundant within Africa, with large amounts of cultural diversity being found not only across different countries but also within single countries. Even though African cultures are widely diverse, it is also, when closely studied, seen to have many similarities. For example, the morals they uphold, their love and respect for their culture as well as the strong respect they hold for the aged and the important, i.e. Kings and Chiefs.

Africa has influenced and been influenced by other continents. This can be portrayed in the willingness to adapt to the ever-changing modern world rather than staying rooted to their static culture. The Westernized few, persuaded by European culture and Christianity, first denied African traditional culture, but with the increase of African nationalism, a cultural recovery occurred.

Task 1 Topic discussion.

Have you ever heard about the term "Cultural Globalization"? What's your attitude towards it? And what's your advice for the recovery of African culture?

____

____

____

____

____

Task 2 Listen to the following recording and then fill in the blanks.①

For hundreds of years, Africans have preserved their history through 1__________. But, some Africans worry that oral traditions will be lost to internet connections and social media. This has led one Nigerian woman to create a mobile phone 2__________, or app, as a way to preserve African folk stories. Elizabeth Kperrun is a businesswoman and fashion designer. She calls her mobile app AfroTalez. The AfroTalez app tells children's stories that teach 3__________. Ms. Kperrun says she wanted to create the app to preserve some of the stories told to her when she was a child in Nigeria.

"Sometimes you can't teach a child something by telling the child, 'Don't do this'. In fact, I think it gave me context. In a story somebody stole something and then something bad happened to them. Alternatively, somebody else did something good and they ended up really happy or really rich."

"Hello children. My name is Liz and I'd like to tell you a story about a tortoise, an elephant, and a hippopotamus. This story will tell you why it's important to go to school so you can 4__________ to be very wise like the tortoise."

AfroTalez is designed for children aged two to ten. The voice of "Aunt Liz" narrates the story, while a full-screen 5__________ appears. An arrow signals when it is time to move on. There are also quizzes on object recognition and counting throughout. "Can you point at Mr. Elephant? No, try again. Good! Find the rope. No, try again... Good!"

Kperrun spoke to her 6__________ to help collect stories for the application. The stories come from an ethnic group of about four million people called the Tiv who live in southeast Nigeria and northwest Cameroon. Ms. Kperrun says she wants to include folktales from other parts of Nigeria in local languages in those areas.

"I want to keep it centered around folk stories. I don't want the popular ones that, let's say, Walt Disney has made really popular... I think it's only 7__________ that we keep certain cultures alive because most of the folk stories are part of the tapestry that keeps cultures together."

Kperrun writes and reads the stories. Her business partner and husband Idamiebi Ilamina-Eremie does the animation. AfroTalez is available for Android users and can be downloaded for free in the Google Play store. So far, AfroTalez has more than 50,000 users. Funding for the

---

① The audio can be accessed here: https://www.tingclass.net/show-8383-313934-1.html?ivk_sa=1024320u.

app has been 8__________. Ms. Kperrun hopes to use a crowdfunding campaign to help fund the next version of AfroTalez to be released this year.

Ms. Kperrun says technology does not have to 9__________ traditions. She says her goal is to combine both new technology and old traditions to keep African culture alive. "Africa is our home. I think 10__________ that we are forgetting things that are really important, things that should be passed on of who we are, and I don't think that's right."

Task 3 Watch the TED talk titled *How Africa can keep rising* and answer the following questions.①

Brief introduction to the speech: African growth is a trend, not a fluke, says economist and former Finance Minister of Nigeria Ngozi Okonjo-Iweala. In this refreshingly candid and straightforward talk, Okonjo-Iweala describes the positive progress on the continent and outlines eight challenges African nations still need to address in order to create a better future.

1. According to the speaker, what were the things that the African countries did right and what did they do wrong in the past decade?

____

____

2. What is the speaker's attitude towards corruption fight?

____

____

Task 4 Understand Africa through film.

The Gods Must Be Crazy is a 1980 South African comedy film written and directed by Jamie Uys. Financed only from local sources, it is the most commercially successful release in the history of South Africa's film industry. Originally released in 1980, the film is the first in *The Gods Must Be Crazy* series. It is followed by one official sequel, *The Gods Must Be Crzay II*, released by Columbia Pictures.

Talk about problems of the so-called modern civilization which are reflected in this film.

____

____

① The video can be accessed here: https://www.ted.com/talks/ngozi_okonjo_iweala_how_africa_can_keep_rising#t-905068.

Lead in

The African continent is the home to some of the world's fast-growing economies. Many of these developing economies rely on crude oil for foreign exchange earnings. These top oil-producing countries include Nigeria, Libya, Algeria, Angola, Egypt and so on (see Figure 3-1) .

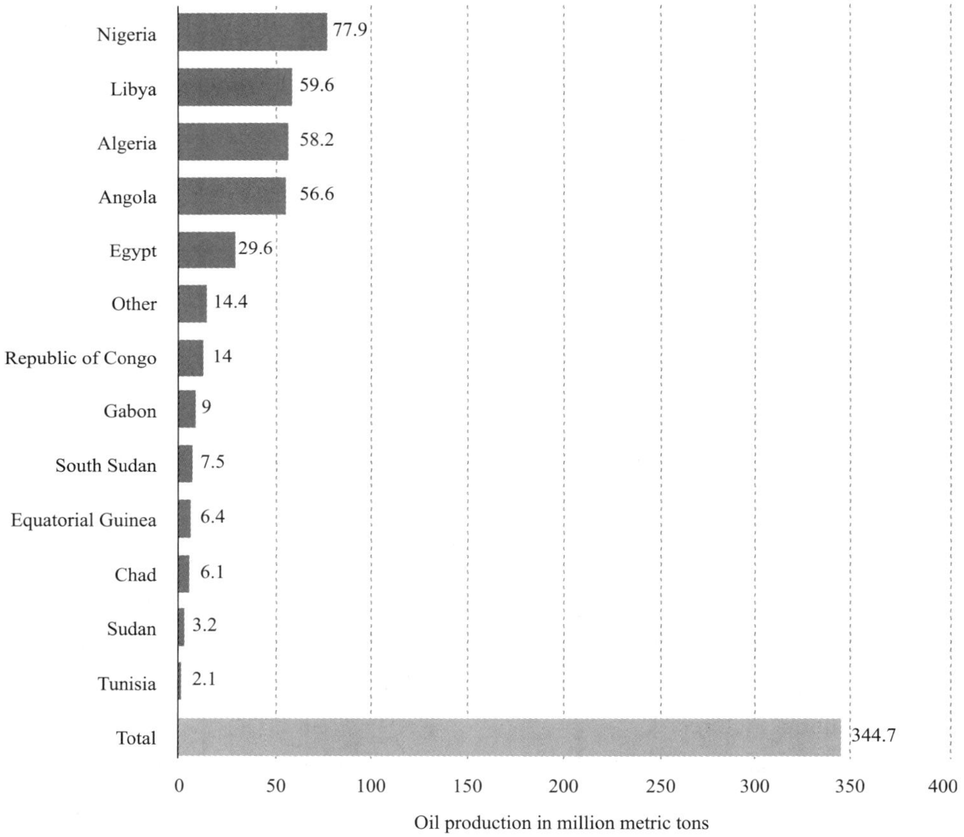

Figure 3-1 Oil production in Africa as of 2021, by country[①]

① Statista. (2022-08-03)[2022-08-20]. https://www.statista.com/statistics/1178514/main-oil-producing-countries-in-africa/.

Text A

Emergence of Nigeria as a Political and Economic Entity①

The name Nigeria was proposed by British journalist Flora Shaw in the 1890s. She referred to the area as Nigeria, after the Niger River, which rules much of the country's landscape. The word niger is Latin for black.

Nigeria is a federal constitutional republic comprising 36 states and its Federal Capital Territory, Abuja. Nigeria is located in West Africa and shares land borders with the Republic of Benin in the west, Chad and Cameroon in the east, and Niger in the north. Its coast in the south lies on the Gulf of Guinea in the Atlantic Ocean.

Nigerians derive from over 250 ethnic groups and languages. Though there are multiple ethnic groups in Nigeria, economic factors result in significant mobility of Nigerians of multiple ethnic and religious backgrounds to reside in territories in Nigeria that are outside their ethnic or religious background, resulting in the intermixing of the various ethnic and religious groups, especially in Nigeria's cities. The largest groups are the Hausa in the north, the Yoruba in the southwest and the Igbo (or Ibo) in the southeast, who account for around a fifth of the population each. The languages of these three groups can therefore be used in government. Other large groups include the Ijaw in the east and the Fulani in the north. Regarding religion, Nigeria is divided roughly in half between Christians, who live mostly in the southern and central parts of the country, and Muslims, concentrated mostly in the northern and southwestern regions. A minority of the population practice religions indigenous to Nigeria, such as those native to Igbo and Yoruba peoples.

The geographical entity now known as Nigeria became a single country in 1914 under British colonial rule following the amalgamation of what was then known as the Southern and Northern Protectorates. Consequently, the history of modern Nigeria is just a little over 100 years. However, the history of the several nationalities making up Nigeria dates back several 1,000 years. As Crowder observed, "Although Nigeria was the creation of European ambitions and rivalries in West Africa, it would be an error to assume that its peoples had little history before its final boundaries were negotiated by Britain, France and Germany at the turn of the twentieth century. Within its frontiers were the great kingdom of Kanem-Borno with a known history of more than a 1,000 years; the Sokoto Caliphate which for nearly a 100 years before

---

① Nigeria. [2022-04-08]. https://familypedia.fandom.com/wiki/Nigeria#Culture.
ADEGBITE O. Perspectives on Industrial Development in Nigeria: Issues, Challenges and Hard Choinces. Switzerland: Springer Cham, 2021.

its conquest by Britain had ruled most of the savannah of northern Nigeria; the kingdoms of Ife and Benin whose art had become recognized as amongst the most accomplished in the world; the Yoruba Empire of Oyo which had once been the most powerful of the states of the Guinea Coast; and the city states of the Niger Delta which had grown partly in response to European demands for slaves and later palm oil; the largely politically decentralized Igbo speaking peoples of the south-east who had produced the famous Igbo-Ukwu bronzes and terracottas; and the small tribes of the Plateau some of whom are descendants of the people who created the famous Nok terracottas."

Nigeria is often referred to as the "Giant of Africa", owing to the large population and economic achievements in comparison to countries that surround this land. With approximately 212 million inhabitants in 2021, Nigeria is the most populous country in Africa and the seventh most populous country in the world. Nigeria has one of the largest populations of youth in the world. One in five people in sub-Saharan Africa is Nigerian. The UN expects there is going to be around 440 million Nigerians in 2050. Its economy has been growing at an average rate of around 7% a year over the past decade. It is rich in resources, especially oil. The country's oil reserves have played a major role in its growing wealth and influence. It has energetic entrepreneurs and aspirations to be the tech hub of Africa, boasting startups such as Konga and Jumia, budding Nigerian Alibabas. In other industries it has giants such as Dangote Cement, which plans to list in London — as the big oil firm, Seplat, did — and is likely to become part of the portfolio of many pension funds. Growing numbers of foreigners wanting to invest in Africa's rise will buy Nigerian stocks; after Johannesburg, Lagos has the biggest, most liquid market in the region. Nigeria is considered to be an emerging market by the World Bank and has been identified as a regional power in Africa. In 2014, Nigeria's economy (GDP) became the largest in Africa, worth more than $500 billion, and overtook South Africa to become the world's 21st largest economy. By 2050, Nigeria is expected to become one of the world's top 20 economies.

The country may be a giant, but it is still poor: Nigeria ranks 153rd out of 187 countries in the UN's Human Development Index. Despite the rapid growth of recent years, unemployment remains high and the number of people in poverty has actually increased. Even with the revised figures, GDP per head is only $2,700; South Africans are more than twice as rich. Whereas large parts of South Africa have a rich country's infrastructure, Nigeria suffers from clogged traffic and chronic power cuts. Lack of development is helping to breed an insurgency in the mainly Muslim north and stokes violence elsewhere that creates no-go areas for foreigners. And the numbers also show its growth rate is slipping. To absorb the millions of young people pouring into the labor market, Nigeria requires the sustained double-digit growth that China has shown to be possible. To achieve that some sort of reform is needed. So let Nigeria celebrate its new-found status for a moment. And then let it get on with the task of living up to being Africa's Number One.

Exercises

Task 1 Match the three ethnic groups on the left with the descriptions on the right.

1. Hausa	A. largest in the southeast
2. Igbo	B. predominant in the southwest
3. Yoruba	C. predominant in the north

Task 2 Answer the following questions according to the information from text A.

1. What is the origin of the name Nigeria?

____

____

2. What are the large ethnic groups in Nigeria?

____

____

3. What are the religions practiced in Nigeria?

____

____

4. According to Crowder, why would it be an error to assume that Nigerians had little history before the twentieth century?

____

____

5. Why is Nigeria often referred to as the "Giant of Africa"?

____

____

Task 3 Translate the following sentences into Chinese.

1. Nigeria is located in West Africa and shares land borders with the Republic of Benin in the west, Chad and Cameroon in the east, and Niger in the north.

____

____

2. The geographical entity now known as Nigeria became a single country in 1914 under British colonial rule following the amalgamation of what was then known as the Southern and Northern Protectorates.

____

____

3. Despite the rapid growth of recent years, unemployment remains high and the number of people in poverty has actually increased.

____

____

Task 4 Critical thinking enhancement.

Have you ever heard of Nollywood? Nollywood, the Nigerian movie industry, is one of the largest film industries in the world based on the quantity of films produced. The other two famous film industries are India's Bollywood and USA's Hollywood. What is the role of Nollywood in Nigeria's development?

____

____

____

____

____

Text B

Discover Algeria in a Nutshell[①]

Algeria is a large, predominantly Muslim country of North Africa. From the Mediterranean coast, along which most of its people live, Algeria extends southward deep into the heart of the Sahara, a forbidding desert where the Earth's hottest surface temperatures have been recorded and which constitutes more than four-fifths of the country's area. The Sahara and its extreme climate dominate the country. The contemporary Algerian novelist Assia Djebar has highlighted the environs, calling her country "a dream of sand" .

History, language, customs, and an Islamic heritage make Algeria an integral part of the Maghrib and the larger Arab world, but the country also has a sizable Amazigh (Berber) population, with links to that cultural tradition. Once the breadbasket of the Roman Empire, the territory now comprising Algeria was ruled by various Arab-Amazigh dynasties from the 8th through the 16th century, when it became part of the Ottoman Empire. The decline of the Ottomans was followed by a brief period of independence that ended when France launched a war of conquest in 1830.

By 1847 the French had largely suppressed Algerian resistance to the invasion and the following year made Algeria a *département* of France. French colonists modernized Algeria's agricultural and commercial economy but lived apart from the Algerian majority, enjoying social and economic privileges extended to few non-Europeans. Ethnic resentment, fueled by revolutionary politics introduced by Algerians who had lived and studied in France, led to a widespread nationalist movement in the mid-20th century. A war of independence ensued (1954–1962).

Negotiations ended the conflict and led to Algerian independence, and most Europeans left the country. Although the influence of the French language and culture in Algeria remained strong, since independence the country consistently has sought to regain its Arab and Islamic heritage. At the same time, the development of oil and natural gas and other mineral deposits in the Algerian interior brought new wealth to the country and prompted a modest rise in the standard of living. In the early 21st century Algeria's economy was among the largest in Africa. Partially because education is more accessible to the common Algerian than it was ever

---

① CHANDERLI A K. Algeria. (2022-03-15) [2022-04-16]. https://www.britannica.com/place/Algeria. DETLEF S. Algeria — Culture, Customs and Social Etiquette. (2013-07-01) [2022-04-18]. https://www.24hourtranslation.com/algeria-culture-customs-and-social-etiquette.html.

before, the present Algerian society continues to strive to modernize and enter the world club of developed countries.

Algerian culture and society were profoundly affected by 130 years of colonial rule, by the bitter independence struggle, and by the subsequent broad mobilization policies of post-independence regimes. A transient, nearly rootless society has emerged, whose cultural continuity has been deeply undermined. There has been a contradiction, however, between the government's various populist policies — which have called for the radical modernization of society as well as the cultivation of the country's Arab Islamic heritage — and traditional family structure. Seemingly, Algerians have been caught between a tradition that no longer commands their total loyalty and a modernism that is attractive yet fails to satisfy their psychological and spiritual needs.

Despite efforts to modernize Algerian society, the pull of traditional values remains strong. Whether in the city or countryside, the daily life of the average Algerian is permeated with the atmosphere of Islam, which has become identified with the concept of an autonomous Algerian people and of resistance to what many Algerians perceive as a continued Western imperialism. Practiced largely as a set of social prescriptions and ethical attitudes, Islam in Algeria has more characteristically been identified with supporting traditional values than serving a revolutionary ideology.

In particular, the influential Muslim clergy has opposed the emancipation of women. Algerians traditionally consider the family — headed by the husband — to be the basic unit of society, and women are expected to be obedient and provide support to their husbands. As in most parts of the Arab world, men and women in Algeria generally have constituted two separate societies, each with its own attitudes and values. Daily activities and social interaction normally take place only between members of the same gender. Marriage in this milieu is generally considered a family affair rather than a matter of personal preference, and parents typically arrange marriages for their children, although this custom is declining as Algerian women take on a greater role in political and economic life. Some women continue to wear veils in public because traditionally minded Algerian Muslims consider it improper for a woman to be seen by men to whom she is not related. The practice of veiling has in fact increased since independence, especially in urban areas, where there is a greater chance of contact with nonrelatives.

The following information might be helpful to do business with Algerians. The Algerian are warm and welcoming and like to entertain guests. They greet a guest or a visitor by a genial handshake. In case of women, because it is the individual's choice to shake hands with a man or not, it is best to wait and see if the woman extends her hand herself. After the handshake, people inquire after the health and well-being of others present. The focus issue for the meeting should be mentioned after one has given his/her introduction. It is not appropriate to come directly to the point. Using first names isn't offensive but doing so depends on the level of intimacy and frankness of all involved. A formal occasion or meeting requires attendees to address people by their last names. Giving a gift shows your love and concern. Algerians love to be given gifts and it is the best way to form a bond. Algerians are very friendly and they like to build a relationship based on trust and respect. They are even friendly with people with whom they interact only for business. Often they try to create an informal relationship by holding hands longer than necessary or using other similar physical gestures to show affection. One must accept the practice as nothing unusual. They must not feel humiliation or an effort to snub them. Outsiders must always show respect for their opinions. Business cards should preferably be typed in Arabic or French. Scheduling appointments is important before planning to meet; similarly scheduling a meeting on short notice is neither customary nor welcome.

Exercises

Task 1 Use the proper forms of the words in the table to complete the following sentences. You may not use any of the words in the table more than once.

constitute	suppress	fuel	subsequent	predominantly
snub	permeate	identify	emancipation	prescription

1. The economic boom was ________ by easy credit.
2. Love of peace is the ________ feeling of many people today.
3. Volunteers ________ more than 95% of the center's work force.
4. The smell of roast chicken ________ the air.
5. The reproduction and growth of cancerous cells can be ________ by radiation.
6. ________ events confirmed our doubts.
7. I could speak their language and ________ with their problems because I had been there myself.
8. The aim of this struggle is to guarantee freedom and ________ for all oppressed groups.
9. The doctor gave me a ________ for antibiotics.
10. I tried to be friendly, but she ________ me completely.

Task 2 Answer the following questions according to the information from text B.

1. Which coast do most of Algerian people live along?

____

____

2. What brought new wealth to Algeria and prompted a modest rise in the standard of living since independence?

____

____

3. What profoundly affected Algerian culture and society?

____

____

Task 3 Translate the following sentences into Chinese.

1. French colonists modernized Algeria's agricultural and commercial economy but lived apart from the Algerian majority, enjoying social and economic privileges extended to few non-Europeans.

____

____

2. Partially because education is more accessible to the common Algerian than it was ever before, the present Algerian society continues to strive to modernize and enter the world club of developed countries.

____

____

3. Practiced largely as a set of social prescriptions and ethical attitudes, Islam in Algeria has more characteristically been identified with supporting traditional values than serving a revolutionary ideology.

____

____

Task 4 Please write an essay of 300 words in response to the following question.

China and Algeria established the comprehensive strategic partnership in 2014, and signed a memorandum of understanding on cooperation under the framework of the BRI during the Beijing Summit of the Forum on China–Africa Cooperation held in 2018. Which fields should be attached more importance to when these two countries enhance their cooperation?

Text C

Ancient Egyptian Civilization[①]

Overview

• Egyptian civilization developed along the Nile River in large part because the river's annual flooding ensured reliable, rich soil for growing crops.

• Repeated struggles for political control of Egypt showed the importance of the region's agricultural production and economic resources.

• The Egyptians kept written records using a writing system known as hieroglyphics.

• Egyptian rulers used the idea of divine kingship and constructed monumental architecture to demonstrate and maintain power.

• Ancient Egyptians developed wide-reaching trade networks along the Nile, in the Red Sea, and in the Near East.

Early Egypt

Much of the history of Egypt is divided into three "kingdom" periods — Old, Middle, and New — with shorter intermediate periods separating the kingdoms. The term "intermediate" here refers to the fact that during these times Egypt was not a unified political power, and thus was in between powerful kingdoms. Even before the Old Kingdom period, the foundations of Egyptian civilization were being laid for thousands of years, as people living near the Nile increasingly focused on sedentary agriculture, which led to urbanization and specialized, non-agricultural economic activity.

Evidence of human habitation in Egypt stretches back tens of thousands of years. It was only in about 6000 BCE, however, that widespread settlement began in the region. Around this time, the Sahara Desert expanded. Some scientists think this expansion was caused by a slight shift in the tilt of the Earth. Others have explored changing rainfall patterns, but the specific causes are not entirely clear. The most important result of this expansion of the Sahara for human civilization was that it pushed humans closer to the Nile River in search of reliable water sources.

Apart from the delta region, most settlement in the Nile Valley was confined to within a few miles of the river itself. The Nile River flooded annually; this flooding was so regular that the

① Ancient Egyptian Civilization. [2022-04-22]. https://www.khanacademy.org/humanities/wold-history-beginnings/ancient-egypt-hittites/a/egypt-article.

ancient Egyptians set their three seasons — Inundation (or Flooding), Growth, and Harvest — around it.

This annual flooding was vital to agriculture because it deposited a new layer of nutrient-rich soil each year. In years when the Nile did not flood, the nutrient level in the soil was seriously depleted, and the chance of food shortages increased greatly. Food supplies had political effects, as well, and periods of drought probably contributed to the decline of Egyptian political unity at the ends of both the Old and Middle Kingdoms.

Although we do not know the specific dates and events, most scholars who study this period believe that sometime around the year 3100 BCE, a leader named either Narmer or Menes — sources are unclear on whether these were the same person — united Egypt politically when he gained control of both Upper and Lower Egypt.

Somewhat confusingly, when you look at a map of this area, Lower Egypt is the delta region in the north, and Upper Egypt refers to the southern portion of the country, which is upriver from the delta. You may encounter this terminology when reading about rivers in history, so a good trick is to remember that rivers flow downhill, so the river is lower toward its end at the sea and higher closer to its source!

After political unification, divine kingship, or the idea that a political ruler held his power by favor of a god or gods — or that he was a living incarnation of a god — became firmly established in Egypt. For example, in the mythology that developed around unification, Narmer was portrayed as Horus, a god of Lower Egypt, where Narmer originally ruled. He conquered Set, a god of Upper Egypt. This mythologized version of actual political events added legitimacy to the king's rule.

The use of hieroglyphics — a form of writing that used images to express sounds and meanings — likely began in this period. As the Egyptian state grew in power and influence, it was better able to mobilize resources for large-scale projects and required better methods of record-keeping to organize and manage an increasingly large state. During the Middle Kingdom, Egyptians began to write literature, as well. Some writing was preserved on stone or clay, and some was preserved on papyrus, a paper-like product made from reed fiber. Papyrus is very fragile, but due to the hot and dry climate of Egypt, a few papyrus documents have survived. Hieroglyphic writing also became an important tool for historians studying ancient Egypt once it was translated in the early 1800s.

As rulers became more powerful, they were better able to coordinate labor and resources to construct major projects, and more people required larger supplies of food. Projects to improve agricultural production, such as levees and canals became more important. Irrigation practices consisted of building mud levees — which were walls of compacted dirt that directed the annual flooding onto farmland and kept it away from living areas — and of digging canals to direct water to fields as crops were growing.

Elites, those individuals who were wealthy and powerful, began building larger tombs which were precursors to the pyramids. These tombs represented a growing divide between the elite and common people in Egyptian society. Only the wealthy and important could afford and be considered as deserving of such elaborate burials.

Old Kingdom Egypt

During the Old Kingdom period, Egypt was largely unified as a single state; it gained in complexity and expanded militarily. Old Kingdom rulers built the first pyramids, which were both tombs and monuments for the kings who had them built. Building monumental architecture — such as the Great Pyramid and the Sphinx in Giza, and temples for different gods — required a centralized government that could command vast resources.

The builders of the pyramids were not enslaved people but peasants, working on the pyramids during the farming off-season. These peasants worked alongside specialists like stone cutters, mathematicians, and priests. As a form of taxation, each household was required to provide a worker for these projects, although the wealthy could pay for a substitute. This demonstrates both the power of the state to force people to provide labor and also the advantages enjoyed by elites, who could buy their way out of providing labor.

Egyptians also began to build ships, constructed of wooden planks tied together with rope and stuffed with reeds, to trade goods such as ebony, incense, gold, copper, and Lebanese cedar — which was particularly important for construction projects — along maritime routes.

Middle Kingdom

The Middle Kingdom saw Egypt unified again as kings found ways to take back power from regional governors. From the Middle Kingdom era forward, Egyptian kings often kept well-trained standing armies. The ability of the Egyptian state to create and maintain a standing military force and to build fortifications showed that it had regained control of substantial resources.

Political fragmentation led to the Second Intermediate Period. The precise dates are unclear; even though writing allowed for more events to be recorded, most things still were not, and many more records have been lost or destroyed.

Taking advantage of this political instability in Egypt, the Hyksos appeared around 1650 BCE. They were a Semitic people, meaning they spoke a language that originated in the Middle East, which indicated that they were not native to Egypt. The Hyksos imposed their own political rulers but also brought many cultural and technological innovations, such as bronze working and pottery techniques, new breeds of animals and new crops, the horse and chariot, the composite bow, battle-axes, and fortification techniques for warfare.

New Kingdom

Around 1550 BCE, the New Kingdom period of Egyptian history began with the expulsion of the Hyksos from Egypt and the restoration of centralized political control. This period was Egypt's most prosperous time and marked the peak of its power.

Also in this period, Hatshepsut, Egypt's most famous female ruler, established trade networks that helped build the wealth of Egypt and commissioned hundreds of construction projects and pieces of statuary, as well as an impressive mortuary temple at Deir el-Bahri. She also ordered repairs to temples that had been neglected or damaged during the period of Hyksos rule.

The term pharaoh, which originally referred to the king's palace, became a form of address for the king himself during this period, further emphasizing the idea of divine kingship. Religiously, the pharaohs associated themselves with the god Amun-Ra, while still recognizing other deities.

In the mid-1300s BCE, one pharaoh attempted to alter this tradition when he chose to worship Aten exclusively and even changed his name to Akhenaten in honor of that god. Some scholars interpret this as the first instance of monotheism, or the belief in a single god. This change did not survive beyond Akhenaten's rule, however.

New Kingdom Egypt reached the height of its power under the pharaohs Seti Ⅰ and Ramesses Ⅱ, who fought to expand Egyptian power against the Libyans to the west and the Hittites to the north. The city of Kadesh on the border between the two empires was a source of conflict between the Egyptians and the Hittites, and they fought several battles over it, ultimately agreeing to the world's first known peace treaty.

Third Intermediate Period

The costs of war, increased droughts, famine, civil unrest, and official corruption ultimately fragmented Egypt into a collection of locally-governed city-states. Taking advantage of this political division, a military force from the Nubian kingdom of Kush in the south conquered and united Lower Egypt, Upper Egypt, and Kush. The Kushites were then driven out of Egypt in 670 BCE by the Assyrians, who established a client state (a political entity that is self-governing but pays tribute to a more powerful state) in Egypt.

In 656 BCE, Egypt was again reunited and broke away from Assyrian control. The country experienced a period of peace and prosperity until 525 BCE, when the Persian king Cambyses defeated the Egyptian rulers and took the title of Pharaoh for himself, along with his title as king of Persia.

Exercises

Task 1 Answer the following questions according to the information from text C.

1. Why was the Nile River essential to Egyptian civilization?

____

____

2. How might a writing system like hieroglyphics have helped rulers gain and maintain political power?

____

____

3. What was one difference between common people and elites?

____

____

4. How did rulers use religion to support their positions?

____

____

5. Why do you think Egypt was invaded so frequently throughout its history?

____

____

Task 2 Translate the following sentences into Chinese.

1. The term "intermediate" here refers to the fact that during these times Egypt was not a unified political power, and thus was in between powerful kingdoms.

____

____

2. Building monumental architecture — such as the Great Pyramid and the Sphinx in Giza, and temples for different gods — required a centralized government that could command vast

resources.

____

____

3. The costs of war, increased droughts, famine, civil unrest, and official corruption ultimately fragmented Egypt into a collection of locally-governed city-states.

____

____

Task 3 Expanded learning: *Egypt-Quest for Eternity*.①

The documentary *Egypt-Quest for Eternity* is about ancient Egypt, its temples, paintings and art, and how these old treasures are being endangered by modern civilization. Also shown are the Nile River, the Luxor and Karnak temples, the Sphynx, the Great Pyramids of Giza, the river path to the Land of the Dead, the pharaohs and queens' tombs, as well as egyptologists' interpretation of Ancient Egypt mysteries.

____

____

____

____

____

① The video can be accessed here: https://www.bilibili.com/video/BV1aJ411z7TJ?from=search&seid=9317846505811512677&spm_id_from=333.337.0.0.

Practical Tips

How to Win in Africa[①]

In this episode of *the McKinsey Podcast*, Simon London speaks with McKinsey senior partners Acha Leke and Georges Desvaux about the opportunity before companies to develop and grow their businesses in Africa.

Podcast transcript (excerpts)

Simon London: Hello, and welcome to this edition of *the McKinsey Podcast,* with me, Simon London. When you think about Africa, what comes to mind? It's hard not to be swayed by news reports of crisis and conflict. But as we'll hear today, another narrative is starting to take hold. It's one centered on rising incomes, urbanization, technology and better government. It's a story told compellingly in a new book, *Africa's Business Revolution*, coauthored by McKinsey partners Acha Leke and Georges Desvaux and McKinsey alumnus Mutsa Chironga. I was lucky enough to catch up with Acha and Georges in person for a wide-ranging conversation about Africa's business scene today, how and why it's changing, and why Africa might just be the world's next great growth market. Georges and Acha, welcome to the podcast, thanks for being here.

Acha Leke: Thanks for having us.

Georges Desvaux: Delighted to be with you.

Simon London: Imagine for a minute that I'm running a big multinational company. I've got options to invest in many different parts of the world. Why should I prioritize Africa? Why should I be thinking about scaling up in Africa in particular?

Acha Leke: If you're a multinational company, there's no better place to invest in than in Africa. If you think of the continent today, it's young, it's fast growing, and it's urbanizing. Half of Africans are under the age of 19, so if you're taking a long-term, 10-, 20-, 30-year view, where else do you want to be? The continent is going to add another billion or so Africans over the next 20 to 30 years. We'll have the largest working population, larger than China, in 6,000 days. And it's urbanizing, so we're the fastest-urbanizing region in the world. Every year we have 24 million Africans moving to cities. To reach them is not that difficult. You decide to focus on a few critical cities. As you put all that together, when you take a long-term view as a consumer-facing company, it's hard to think of a better place. I'll give an example. In Nigeria

① How to Win in Africa. (2018-11-20) [2022-04-23]. https://www.mckinsey.com/featured-insights/middle-east-and-africa/how-to-win-in-africa.

alone, there are more babies born every year than in the whole of Western Europe. If you're a diaper company, where would you want to be based?

Georges Desvaux: It's a little like thinking about whether (companies) should have gone into China 25 years ago. Having lived in China at the time, you can see the parallels playing out in Africa. It's roughly the same population but also what I find quite extraordinary is the level of energy, the level of development. When you go to a city like Lagos, you really think you are in China 25 years ago. When you look at this and you look at the energy, the entrepreneurship, the drive, it will probably take a different shape and form, but it will actually develop. There are two differences which I think are very important: in Africa, the young population, as Acha mentioned, will drive the development on a different scale because we'll get to two billion people in the next 20 years. Second is the availability of technology. Where Africa is, contrary to where China was 25 years ago, is actually leapfrogging in many places with technology and that opens up a lot more opportunities that people may not have seen at this stage.

Acha Leke: I'll add one thing that we mentioned in the book — we talked a lot about the population growth. But you also think about the growth of disposable income because what we're finding is there's GDP growth and that's translating into disposable-income growth. When you combine those two factors, it's more like exponential growth than linear growth. There are very few places in the world today where you will really get those two factors coming together that strongly.

Simon London: You two must spend a lot of time talking with clients about Africa and the Africa opportunity. What are some of the misconceptions that you hear as you do that?

Acha Leke: I would say there's a big difference between perception of risk versus the reality on the ground. A lot of clients who are not based on the continent tend to read the news and the sensational headlines you hear. And their view of the risk is quite different from what's on the ground. I used to have a client, a downstream oil company, and they said, "Look, we're in 30 countries. Every year five will blow up, but we don't know which ones. But the other 25 will do great." What they always told me was, "But we love being in Africa because we do very well. And so we're very happy for people out there to think Africa is too risky." They would come into the market, and they would have less competition. There's a big difference between perceived risk and the reality on the ground.

Georges Desvaux: And the other thing that I think people fail to realize is how important Africa already is in terms of the industrial or private sector. It is in fact doing quite well.

Simon London: Just to be devil's advocate, the political risk is very real as you pointed out, Acha. There are certain countries, in any given five-year period [where] there will be more political risk and volatility than there might be in some other regions of the world. How do you respond to that? As a CEO, how do you manage around that?

Acha Leke: Let's be clear — there are risks. Political is one, so we urge our clients simply to think not just from a growth perspective but also combine growth and risk. When you do that you see three very clear sets of countries that emerge. There are the countries that are quite stable and growing fast. And that tends to be the East African and the francophone African countries. So the Rwandas and the Ethiopias of the world, but also you see some countries like Cote d'Ivoire, Morocco, countries like that. Then you have some that are what we call vulnerable growers, so they're still growing but they've been exposed to some of the shocks. The oil shocks affected places like Nigeria and Angola. Then you have a set of countries that have struggled to just grow. Places like South Africa. Those are the three segments, and in the past as an executive looking at the continent you could literally go anywhere and you'd find growth. Now you have to be a lot more granular, a lot more careful because there are pockets of growth where it's more important to really understand the situation on the ground. Because when you find growth, you have to really get a better sense for how the countries are doing but how the sector even is doing in the country you're interested in.

Georges Desvaux: You also have to look at it and say, this is a long-term play. This is a 20-, 30-years play. It's the same as China was 30 years ago, India was 15 years ago. Africa is going to be the next pillar of growth because of demographics, because of the natural resources, because of urbanization. And so what you need to do is you need to build the resilience that enables you to manage the risks that are inherent to those three different types of countries that Acha was talking about in order to make sure you are able to go through and weather the storms at some point. Because you take a country like Nigeria, for example, which many people would say, "Well, it's difficult, it's dangerous, there are risks, there is Boko Haram, there are issues." But there are 180 million inhabitants, with a striving group of entrepreneurs who are really driving very hard to develop their own enterprises, and that's a force that you cannot ignore. And you have that with Nigeria, you have Ethiopia with about 90 million people. You have the whole francophone West Africa, which is another 100 million, so those are massive places where people are really trying hard to develop and build their economies.

Acha Leke: Definitely, I think diversifying your portfolio makes sense. What we've found is the most successful companies have typically been across multiple countries because like I said, you just never know when something could happen. If you look at the multinationals that have been most successful, they've been in ten or more countries and they've been here for a long time. So that's one. But the second thing, which is important, is we've also realized in building these companies that have revenues over a billion dollars, it's very difficult to build a billion-dollar business if you're not in one of three economies. If not in South Africa, Nigeria, or Egypt, it's just very difficult, you just don't have enough scale. As you think about diversifying your portfolio, think also about what is the role that one or many of these three countries will play in that portfolio.

Simon London: Just talk a little bit more about what it takes to win in Africa. The backbone of the book is building for resilience in your strategy, taking that into account. That's clearly a lever. What are the other things that jump out to you? What's the secret sauce?

Acha Leke: Much of the book was focused on what's the secret sauce. We found four elements to that and I'll bring them all together, and we'll talk about each (see Figure 3–2). One was, as Georges talked about, mapping your Africa strategy, which is very much about where to play. Which countries should you play in? Do you want to do what I call a Vodacom strategy? Or do you want a MTN strategy, which is to go across multiple countries at once? You can be very successful at either one, but you need to pick. We always say if you're a consumer-facing company, think cities not countries. So what 20 cities do you want to be in versus what five countries? But that's really about, where do you want to play?

Figure 3–2 Four elements can help companies build a strong business strategy in Africa

(Source: McKinsey Insights executive survey on business in Africa, 2017)

Then after there's innovating a business model. What parts do you want to innovate in? We've seen a number of places who have innovated in products and services. We've seen others who could leverage technology to innovate. So you have to think about is it just driving costs down to really be one of the lowest-cost producers? There's a third element that we've talked about, and that's the resilience. How are you going to build resilience? How do you make sure that you're here for the long term, because you're going to have ups and downs. It's a continent.

There are 54 countries. Through ups and downs, how do you build resilience? And within that is what parts of the value chain do you want to control? We've seen a lot of companies that have been successful have had to insource a lot of work they would typically outsource in other markets because they need to gain control of that. And then fourth is talent. How are you going to build the talent you need? And each of these on its own is not rocket science.

But I'll say two things: where we've seen companies that have been successful, they've been able to be successful across each of those four elements. They've known exactly where to play, they've been very careful about where they're going to innovate, they've been very careful about how they build resilience. And they've found a way to really grow talent. The second thing we found, which is actually quite interesting for us, is the most successful companies have come up at it from wanting to do the right thing for the continent. So it's about what we call doing good by doing well. They didn't come here just because they wanted to make money. They said, "I want to solve a problem and on the back of that I will make money." You have a longer-term perspective. You have a mind-set of really trying to make a difference and improving people's lives. And on the back of that also being a quite successful company for its shareholders.

UNIT 4

Oil-producing Countries in Latin America

Overview

The words "Latin America" are used to describe the group of countries in the American continent where Latin languages are spoken. These countries are all located south of the US–Mexico border, starting with Mexico in North America, extending through Central America and parts of the Caribbean and down into the southernmost tip of South America — the region known as Tierra del Fuego.

Latin America shares elements of historical experience, language and culture. This group of countries have more in common with each other, in many respects, than they do with Canada and the US.①

Task 1 Approach Latin America.

Speaking of Latin America, what would spring to your mind?

____

____

____

____

____

① MCKEOWN M. What Is Latin America? Geography, Language and Culture Explained. (2022-07-05) [2022-08-31]. https://owlcation.com/social-sciences/What-is-Latin-America.

Task 2 Listen to the audio clip about Maya civilization and then fill in the blanks.①

While Europe lingered in the Dark Ages, the splendor of the Maya world was reaching its zenith. Their temples soared hundreds of feet into the heavens. They developed a system of hieroglyphic writing. Works of art and sculpture displayed the Maya's intricate sense of style. And here in Mexico's Yucatán Peninsula, they built the great city of Chichen Itza. The city takes part of its name from the large wells that were its only 1__________ source of water. Spanish records report that live 2__________ were thrown into the sacred well as a 3__________ to the rain god Chaac, who lived in its depth.

The Maya also built this circular building believed to be an observatory. By carefully watching the stars, the Maya developed a 365-day 4__________ and could even predict solar eclipses.

It was the Itza who built the city's most famous building, a pyramid the Spanish called "El Castillo" or the 5__________. This 79-foot pyramid has a total of 365 steps, the same number as the days in a solar year. And it guards another secret, testament to the Maya's skill at math and 6__________. Twice a year, on the day of the spring and autumn equinoxes, a shadow falls on El Castillo in the shape of a serpent. As the sun sets, the snake appears to 7__________ the steps of the pyramid until it finally joins the serpent's head at the base of the staircase.

A bustling trading center past the year 1,000, Chichen Itza 8__________ long after other Mayan cities have been 9__________. But eventually, it likely fell victim to the same forces that felled other Mayan cities, a combination of 10__________ and a top-heavy class of royals, whose costly wars and lavish rituals overtaxed the Maya people.

Sometime in the 1400s, the people of Chichen Itza abandoned their city to the jungle. But today, its imposing ruins still stand amid the rainforest, an impressive and enduring monument to the proud Maya civilization that built it.

Task 3 Watch the video about Aztec civilization and decide whether the statements are true or false.②

1. The city of Tenochtitlan was located atop a volcano. ( )
2. The Aztecs sacrificed human being to appease their gods. ( )
3. When the Spanish conquistadors first arrived, the Aztec people believed that Cortes was actually a god in human form. ( )
4. The Aztecs had immune resistance to smallpox but the Spanish didn't. ( )

---

① The audio can be accessed here: https://www.tingclass.net/show-9849-378550-1.html?gfh.

② The video can be accessed here: https://v.qq.com/x/page/i01538j0ixx.html.

Task 4 Please write an essay of 300 words to discuss the following issue.

Latin America has a vibrant culture that is all its own. Rio Carnival and Mexican food are two representatives. Rio Carnival is the greatest show on Earth and the biggest event of the Brazilian cultural calendar, while Mexican food is well-known for its exotic flavor. Using Rio Carnival and Mexican food as examples, write an essay to discuss in what ways Latin American culture is a fusion of indigenous American, African and European traditions.

Lead in

Do some research and find out information about the major oil-producing countries in Latin America. Finish the following table:

Rank	Country	Production	Top oil and gas companies
1			
2			
3			
4			

Text A

How Soccer Came to Define Brazil[①]

It took less than four decades for Carlos Drummond de Andrade, Brazil's mid-century poet laureate, to get an answer to his question: "There is no Brazil. By any chance, are there Brazilians?" Milton Nascimento's much-recorded song "Here Is the Football Nation" replied, "At the match". It was, from the 1960s onwards, a commonplace of Brazilian culture that football was the national ritual. When the Seleção took the field at the World Cup and over 95 percent of the population were watching them on television, Brazil existed in a more complete way than at any other moment. This was not just a symbolic practice; the demands of football could produce tangible material change too. The 1970 World Cup in Mexico was not only the occasion of Brazil's third, and most scintillating, victory, but also, to ensure nationwide coverage of the games, the first time that a comprehensive north–south telecommunications infrastructure had been built, just one of the many ways in which the Brazilian state has tried to use football to create the nation.

The relentless demands of industrialized warfare have been a powerful catalyst for the creation of national state institutions and a collective sense of national identity, but Brazil never experienced this. Although its military was kept busy fighting a grueling 19th-century war with its Paraguayan neighbors, suppressing independent ex-slave communities in the northeast, putting down a rash of mutinies, regional rebellions, and revolts, and even sending a brigade to fight on the Allied side in Italy in the closing years of the Second World War, none of these

① GOLDBLATT D. Futebol Nation: The Story of Brazil through Soccer. New York: Nation Books, 2014.

conflicts could serve as a crucible of national myth, heroic triumph, or collective fortitude. Given Brazil's calamitously low level of literacy, the creation of a national public sphere through a shared language and literature was not a plausible strategy either.

In this light, Carlos Drummond de Andrade's apparent flippancy belies a profound problem for Brazilian nationalists of the early 20th century. At the most protean moment of Brazil's search to define itself, the answer could not simply be imposed from above on white, literate, and elite terms. Brazil henceforth would have to incorporate some notion of its African demographics, its complex ethnicities, and the non-literate tastes and practices of its emerging urban popular classes. Brazil was, in actual fact, rich in precisely these cultural forms: popular music from choro to the samba and their accompanying dances and carnivals; candomblé, the generic term for African religious and spiritual practices forged from the hybrid of African cultures compressed under slavery; umbanda, the emerging urban form of candomblé that actively mixed African spirits and Catholic saints, pagan ritual and the Roman sacraments. Yet despite the various attempts made by Brazil's elite to appropriate these forms, and to integrate at some level the African contribution to Brazilian life, they did not carry a sense of modernity. On the contrary, they remained rooted in deeply antiquated cultures. Brazilian nationalism required a cultural practice that could encompass the full spectrum of the nation's complex social and racial hierarchies, and that acknowledged the nation's past but set it on a course for the future. Football, especially in its initial association with Britain, the most modern nation of the time, provided just that. It was in this context that the game, as a physical bodily practice, as a collective ritual, as a carnivalesque spectacular and as a historical narrative, open to all Brazilians, acquired its status in the national pantheon; a position solidified by the global success and poetic acclaim of the national team.

Although football was introduced by the British in São Paulo, and initially played by a predominantly expatriate body of players, it is remarkable how swiftly and completely these influences were overtaken. By the end of the First World War, just 20 years after the first recorded games had been played in São Paulo, the British influence had dwindled to almost nothing. Portuguese vernacular rapidly replaced the remnants of English in the game's vocabulary. Corinthians, the team of working-class São Paulo, retained their Anglo-Hellenic name, but the gentlemanly, amateur ethos of elite British sports culture was on its last legs and by the end of the 1930s it had collapsed altogether. British football, represented by touring professional teams, was already seen as profoundly different from the emerging Brazilian style of play. Over the next half-century, as well as being the most popular participatory sport, with the biggest crowds and the overwhelming favorite of media audiences of all kinds, football would become a subject of inquiry and depiction in almost every form of Brazilian popular culture and high art.

Whereas the response of the visual arts in 20th-century Britain to football can be boiled down to a single Lowry canvas, football has appeared in the oeuvre of dozens of Brazil's leading artists — from the nationalist surrealism of Cândido Portinari to the abstract geometries of Ivan Serpa to the pop art of Claudio Tozzi. Its writers and novelists have, again and again, found space for the game in their literary landscapes: from Mário de Andrade's *Macunaíma*, to José Lins do Rego's epic saga of life on Rio's periphery, *Água-mãe*, from the urbane and witty *Crônicas* of Clarice Lispector to the sharp short stories of Edilberto Coutinho's *Maracanã, Adeus*. The game has also been a thread and connector across the many spheres of Brazilian life. João Cabral Melo Neto was a diplomat who wrote poetry and his poetry featured Pelé. Pelé, a footballer, has gone on to be a businessman, the minister of culture, and a singer and composer. The composer Ary Barroso crossed over into football commentary and then to municipal politics. Politicians regularly seek the presidency of clubs, while club presidents try to make the transition to formal politics. The crowd can become musicians, while musicians have endlessly written and composed songs for players and clubs. Poets and dramatists commentate on football. Football commentators like Washington Rodrigues and João Saldanha have become coaches.

When *Globo*'s leading commentator Galvão Bueno criticizes the Seleção's opponents for a fumble or misplaced pass, he says with a mixture of pity and contempt, "They don't have the same intimacy with the ball." It is a tone that assures you that he and his listeners are quite convinced that whatever its origins, whatever the competition, it is only in Brazil that football is truly at home, sunk deep into the web of meanings and memory that the nation has spun around it.

Exercises

Task 1 Why did the following elements fail to define Brazil?

1. warfare: ______
2. language and literature: ______
3. samba, candomblé and umbanda: ______

Task 2 Answer the following questions according to the information from text A.

1. What does the sentence underlined in paragraph one mean?

______

______

2. When did football begin to be the symbol of Brazil?

____

____

3. Why did football become the symbol of Brazil?

____

____

4. How was the British influence overtaken after football was introduced from Britain to Brazil?

____

____

5. How did football influence art and literary in Brazil?

____

____

Task 3 Translate the following sentences into Chinese.

1. The 1970 World Cup in Mexico was not only the occasion of Brazil's third, and most scintillating, victory, but also, to ensure nationwide coverage of the games, the first time that a comprehensive north–south telecommunications infrastructure had been built, just one of the many ways in which the Brazilian state has tried to use football to create the nation.

____

____

2. Yet despite the various attempts made by Brazil's elite to appropriate these forms, and to integrate at some level the African contribution to Brazilian life, they did not carry a sense of modernity.

____

____

3. It is a tone that assures you that he and his listeners are quite convinced that whatever its origins, whatever the competition, it is only in Brazil that football is truly at home, sunk deep into the web of meanings and memory that the nation has spun around it.

____

____

Task 4 Critical thinking enhancement.

Football is the most important sport in Brazil. It is deeply ingrained in the everyday life and culture of the country — it's a national passion and found everywhere you go. Do some research and write an essay of 300 words about football culture in Brazil.

Text B

Day of the Dead in Mexico[1]

Day of the Dead is an interesting holiday celebrated in central and southern Mexico during the chilly days of November 1 and 2. Even though this coincides with the Catholic holiday called All Souls' & All Saints' Day, the indigenous people have combined this with their own ancient beliefs of honoring their deceased loved ones.

They believe that the gates of heaven are opened at midnight on October 31, and the spirits of all deceased children (angelitos) are allowed to reunite with their families for 24 hours. On November 2, the spirits of the adults come down to enjoy the festivities that are prepared for them.

Traditions, rituals and customs

In most Indian villages, beautiful altars (ofrendas) are made in each home. They are decorated with candles, buckets of flowers (wild marigolds called cempasuchil & bright red cock's combs), mounds of fruit, peanuts, plates of turkey mole, stacks of tortillas and big Day of the Dead breads called pan demuerto. The altar needs to have lots of food, bottles of soda, hot cocoa and water for the weary spirits. Toys and candies are left for the angelitos, and on November 2, cigarettes and shots of mezcal are offered to the adult spirits. Little folk art skeletons and sugar skulls, purchased at open-air markets, provide the final touches.

Day of the Dead is a very expensive holiday for these self-sufficient, rural based, indigenous families. Many spend over two month's income to honor their dead relatives. They believe that happy spirits will provide protection, good luck and wisdom to their families. Ofrenda building keeps the family close.

On the afternoon of November 2, the festivities are taken to the cemetery. People clean tombs, play cards, listen to the village band and reminisce about their loved ones. Tradition keeps the village close.

Origins and history

There were many different ethnic groups living in Mesoamerica in ancient times, as

---

① VILLALBA A.History of Day of the Dead ~ Día de los Muertos. (2019-10-04) [2022-05-14].https://mexicansugarskull.com/pages/history-of-day-of-the-dead-dia-de-los-muertos.
BARBEZAT S. Day of the Dead in Mexico: The Complete Guide. (2019-04-14) [2022-05-14]. https://www.tripsavvy.com/day-of-the-dead-in-mexico-1588764.

there still are today. The various groups had and still have different customs, but they also had many things in common. A belief in an afterlife, which dates back to over 5,000 years ago, was very widespread. In many archaeological sites in Mexico, the ornate way in which people were buried shows evidence of the belief in the afterlife, and the fact that tombs were often constructed beneath the homes where they had lived, meant that deceased loved ones would remain close to their living family members.

The Aztecs believed that there were several planes of existence which were separate but interrelated to the one on which we dwell. They envisioned a world with 13 overworlds or layers of heavens above the earthly terrain and nine underworlds. Each of these levels had its own characteristics and particular gods who ruled it. When someone passed away, it was believed that the place their soul would go to was determined by the manner in which they died. Warriors who died in battle, women who died during childbirth, and victims of sacrifice were considered to be the most fortunate, as they would be rewarded by achieving the highest plane in the afterlife.

The Aztecs had a month-long celebration in which the ancestors were honored and offerings were left to them. This festival took place in the month of August and paid homage to the lord and lady of the underworld, Mictlantecuhtli and his wife Mictlancíhuatl. Other groups had different but similar customs and beliefs.

When the Spaniards arrived in the sixteenth century, they introduced the Catholic faith to the indigenous people of Mesoamerica and did their best to stamp out the native religion. They were only somewhat successful, and the Catholic teachings intermingled with the native beliefs to create new traditions. The festival related to death and celebrating the ancestors was moved to coincide with the Catholic holidays of All Saints' Day (November 1) and All Souls' Day (November 2), and although it is considered a Catholic holiday, it retains various elements that are carried over from the pre-Hispanic celebrations.

Celebrations vary from place to place. Some of the best Day of the Dead destinations include Oaxaca, Patzcuaro and Janitzio in Michoacan, and Mixquic, on the outskirts of Mexico City. Day of the Dead is a continually evolving tradition, and Mexico's proximity to the United States has enhanced the overlap that exists between Halloween and Day of the Dead. Children dress up in costumes and, in the Mexican version of trick-or-treating, go out to pedir Muertos (ask for the dead). In some locations, instead of candy, they'll be given items off the family Day of the Dead altar.

Exercises

Task 1 Use the proper forms of the words in the table to complete the following sentences. You may not use any of the words in the table more than once.

coincide	indigenous	decorate	deceased	weary
transcend	interrelate	stamp out	outskirt	overlap

1. The ________ walkers soothed their aching feet in the sea.
2. The living suburbanization is urban population moved from downtown to ________.
3. This fairy tale and other such stories ________ culture and language.
4. Many of the ________ insects are needed to pollinate the local plants.
5. The identities of the ________ have now been determined.
6. The local government has made a drive to ________ corruption among its staff.
7. Children need to be educated about the way that diet and health ________.
8. The exhibition ________ with the 50th anniversary of his death.
9. They ________ the room with flowers and balloons.
10. The language of science ________ with that of everyday life.

Task 2 Answer the following questions according to the information from text B.

1. When is Day of the Dead celebrated in Mexico?

____

____

2. How are the altars decorated?

____

____

3. What do people do during the festival?

____

____

4. What is the origin of Day of the Dead?

____

____

5. How has the festival evolved?

____

____

Task 3 Translate the following sentences into Chinese.

1. Even though this coincides with the Catholic holiday called All Soul's & All Saint's Day, the indigenous people have combined this with their own ancient beliefs of honoring their deceased loved ones.

____

____

2. In many archaeological sites in Mexico, the ornate way in which people were buried shows evidence of the belief in the afterlife, and the fact that tombs were often constructed beneath the homes where they had lived, meant that deceased loved ones would remain close to their living family members.

____

____

3. When the Spaniards arrived in the sixteenth century, they introduced the Catholic faith to the indigenous people of Mesoamerica and did their best to stamp out the native religion.

____

____

Task 4 Watch the movie *Coco* and summarize the Mexican cultural references in it.

____

____

____

____

____

Text C

Hyperinflation in Venezuela①

Imagine going to the store and finding that nothing has a price tag on it. Instead you take it to the cashier and they calculate the price. What you pay could be twice as much, or more, than an hour earlier. That's if there is even anything left in stock.

This is the economic reality in Venezuela. In 2016, a state of emergency was declared by the government. That year the inflation rate hit 800%. Things have since gone from bad to worse. By 2018 inflation was an estimated 80,000%. It's difficult to say what the rate is now, but Bloomberg's Venezuelan Cafe Con Leche Index, based on the price of a cup of coffee, suggests it is now about 380,000%. About 3 million Venezuelans — a tenth of the population — have fled the country. This is the largest human displacement in Latin American history.

So how did things get so bad? How did inflation become hyperinflation in Venezuela? And how do Venezuelans deal with it?

The cost of goods and the value of currency

What we pay for goods and services reflects not only their cost of production but also of the value of the currency we buy them in. If that currency loses value against the currency the goods are sold in, the price of those goods goes up.

By 2014 the value of Venezuela's currency, the bolívar, and the prosperity of the Venezuelan economy, was highly dependent on oil exports. More than 90% of the country's export earnings came from oil.

These export earnings had enabled the government to pay for social programs intended to combat poverty and inequality. From subsidies for those on low incomes to health services, the government's spending obligations were high.

Then the global price of oil dropped. Foreign demand for the bolívar to buy Venezuelan oil crashed. As the currency's value fell, the cost of imported goods rose. The Venezuelan economy went into crisis.

The solution of Venezuela's government was to print more money.

That might seem silly, but it can keep the economy moving while it gets over a hump caused by a short-term price shock.

---

① CARMODY M. What Caused Hyperinflation in Venezuela: A Rare Blend of Public Ineptitude and Private Enterprise. (2019-02-05) [2022-05-17]. http://theconversation.com/what-caused-hyperinflation-in-venezuela-a-rare-blend-of-public-ineptitude-and-private-enterprise-102483.

The Venezuelan crisis, however, just got worse as the oil price continued to fall, compounded by other factors that reduced Venezuelan oil output. International investors began looking elsewhere, driving the value of the bolívar even lower.

In these conditions, printing more money simply made the problem worse. It added to the supply of currency, pushing the value down even further. As prices rose, the government printed more money to pay its bills. This cycle is what causes hyperinflation.

Playing the currency market

Circumstances like these quickly make saving money in the local currency nonsensical. To protect themselves, Venezuelans started to convert their savings into a more stable currency, like the US dollar. This lowered the value of the bolívar even further.

The government responded by issuing currency controls. It set a fixed exchange rate, to stop the official value of the bolívar dropping against the US dollar, and made it difficult to actually get permission to exchange bolívares into US dollars. The idea was to stabilise the currency by effectively shutting down all currency transactions.

US dollars were still available on the black market, however. This meant going to any number of operators on the streets of downtown Caracas or asking a friend to hook you up. As the crisis deepened, more and more Venezuelans looked to switch their bolívares into US dollars.

This increasing demand meant the black market price for greenbacks rose, creating a difference between the official exchange rate (set by the government) and the unofficial going rate.

With this came new opportunities. In 2014 reports emerged that groups of middle-aged women were crossing the border to use ATMs in Colombia. They could withdraw funds from their Venezuelan accounts as US dollars at the official rate. They could then cross back into Venezuela and exchange the dollars for bolívares at the unofficial rate, making a tidy profit. Government officials able to exchange bolívares for US dollars within Venezuela had their own version of this practice.

This pushed the price of US dollars up, and that of bolívares down, even more. As the crisis deepened increasing numbers of ordinary Venezuelans began to engage in the unofficial currency market.

Sometimes this took the form of taking subsidised Venezuelan goods like food across the border to sell. This earned the sellers foreign currency, but it also exacerbated shortages of goods within the country, driving prices up even further.

Cannot be trusted

By August 2018 the Venezuelan currency was worth so little that it was more prudent to use cash for toilet paper rather than buy toilet paper.

The government tried to get on top of this situation by issuing a currency devaluation. The bolívar was devaluated by 95%, the largest currency devaluation in contemporary world history. The new currency was also tied to the price of oil, an economic experiment designed to show the Venezuelan economy had solid foundations.

By bringing the bolívar's value into line with the reality of what people actually thought it was worth, and showing it was backed by something valuable, oil, the Venezuelan government hoped Venezuelans would believe in their own currency and not exchange it for dollars. This would help stabilise the economy overall.

But within weeks of the devaluation it was clear ordinary Venezuelans had not been convinced.

Hyperinflation is a very difficult hole out of which to climb. Very few economies ever experience it, and it's hard to stop it without massively cutting government spending.

It is easy, then, to see why millions of Venezuelans responded by dealing in the black market or taking their savings, and themselves, out the country altogether.

As the crisis in the country deepens, Venezuelans will have to continue to seek ways to allow them to survive the storm any way they can.

Exercises

Task 1 Answer the following questions according to the information from text C.

1. What was the economic reality in Venezuela from 2016 to 2018?

____

____

2. According to the author, what caused the hyperinflation in Venezuela?

____

____

3. What measures did the government take? Were they helpful to solve the problem?

____

____

4. What were the possible consequences of the hyperinflation?

____

____

Task 2 Translate the following sentences into Chinese.

1. The Venezuelan crisis, however, just got worse as the oil price continued to fall, compounded by other factors that reduced Venezuelan oil output.

____

____

2. This earned the sellers foreign currency, but it also exacerbated shortages of goods within the country, driving prices up even further.

____

____

3. By bringing the bolívar's value into line with the reality of what people actually thought it was worth, and showing it was backed by something valuable, oil, the Venezuelan government hoped Venezuelans would believe in their own currency and not exchange it for dollars.

____

____

Task 3 Critical thinking enhancement.

What lessons can be learned from Venezuela's hyperinflation crisis?

____

____

____

____

____

Practical Tips

How Culture Affects Work Practices in Latin America①

Some global executives would be surprised to learn that many employees in Mexico like to do their jobs in the presence of such religious images as the Virgin of Guadalupe. Their religious devotion is one example of how local culture affects the styles and practices of work in Latin America. Anabella Dávila, professor of management theory and business history at the graduate business school (ITESM) in Monterrey (Mexico), and Marta M. Elvira, academic director of Lexington College in Chicago, have published a book on this phenomenon, entitled *Managing Human Resources in Latin America*. In the chapter titled "Culture and Human Resource Management in Latin America", the two scholars identify the cultural values that determine Human Resources in the region. They show how these factors can determine the success and failure of a business organization.

The company is like a family

The authors define the Latin American business model as a hybrid of globalization and the region's historic traditions. With the exception of Argentina and Costa Rica, those traditions are characterized by large social gaps and a widespread collectivism that has various manifestations. Dávila and Elvira explain that social differences are manifested locally through benevolent, paternalistic leadership. "The senior executive has the personal obligation to protect subordinates, and even take care of the personal needs of workers and their families."

Generally speaking, paternalism involves a "father" who cares for his "sons" by engaging in permissive practices and providing moral support, even if his "sons" wind up being too dependent in many respects throughout their working career. Latin American firms are managed like a family. Latin Americans prefer to depend on someone closer to the center of the organization, and to accept that this authority leads to behavior that avoids conflict and confrontation with one's superiors. Behaving any other way would be interpreted as an offense against one's superiors and colleagues. Doing so would have disciplinary consequences.

On the other hand, "Latin Americans value status within a hierarchy because it indicates social distance between the higher-up and his subordinates," notes the study. Job titles and additional benefits also have a great significance because of the social status that they bring. In Chilean companies, for example, social discrimination exists on the basis of appearance, age and gender, all of which are associated with social status. "Despite this sort of hierarchical

---

① How Culture Affects Work Practices in Latin America. (2005-01-26) [2022-05-18]. https://knowledge.wharton.upenn.edu/article/how-culture-affects-work-practices-in-latin-america/.

status, Latin American companies try to eliminate the existing power distance between directors and subordinates by creating committees that symbolize the egalitarian spirit among all members of the organization," notes the study. It is no easy task to play the role of supervisor, however, because a boss must assume that role without actually behaving as such.

The collective spirit of the workplace is manifested in several ways. First, there is the importance of personal relationships. Latin Americans expect to be treated with courtesy and kindness while at work. Second, there is a sense of loyalty to the primary group. In Mexican companies, "executives know that the survival of their organizations depends more on social and governmental relationships than on any support they get from the country's financial system". Third, popular celebrations play a major role in the workplace, including religious behavior, as noted earlier. This illustrates the hybrid style of management.

The importance of social status

This is the cultural framework that defines Human Resource practices within the Latin American company, especially recruitment and personnel management. For example, social relationships and physical appearance "can explain the cultural content of the glass ceiling in Latin American companies". In Chilean companies, executive selection and promotion generally reflect physical appearance, age and sex, in addition to social contacts, birthplace and other factors.

On the other hand, Latin American corporate training and development divisions suffer significant internal conflict when it comes time to provide more advanced business training. They realize that new management techniques don't always fit in well with local tradition; some practices are rejected by employees. So managers feel obliged to provide formal basic education and technical training whenever they modernize work procedures. "The shortage of technical knowledge, formal education, and skills for analysis and communication represent serious obstacles for Mexican workers," says the study. Moreover, Latin American companies usually devote only a small part of their budget to training.

When it comes to compensation and recognition, family also plays a central role. Not surprisingly, the quality of family life cushions workers from recurrent economic crises. In Mexico, work is considered an obligation and way to enjoy the important things in life, including family. If Mexicans had a choice, they would not work. However, the research should be viewed cautiously, the authors warn, because the culture of work varies significantly according to age, socio-economic level, and educational achievement. Some studies discovered that "manufacturing plants in Mexico made major cuts in their expatriate staffs, and found young, bilingual talent with managerial skills and university degrees (to replace them). Young managers accepted modern methods of management and production more readily than older managers did".

Dávila and Elvira warn that individual financial compensation can stigmatize a worker as a "favorite" of management. The worker can wind up being rejected by the group, with grave consequences. In contrast, highly valued benefits for top executives confer extra status — including luxury cars, and private-school tuition for their children.

It is also important to recognize the loyalty of employees by establishing ceremonies that honor their seniority. Many benefits, including vacations and retirement benefits, involve ceremonial recognition. However, Dávila and Elvira warn about linking compensation to formal evaluation of workers' performance. Given the low level of confrontation between managers and their subordinates, the results of that sort of evaluation are rarely used.

Compensation usually comes in the form of fixed salary. Only multinational companies and large Latin American firms provide variable compensation based on corporate performance. Fixed salaries are more appropriate in a hierarchical and individualistic system where more value is placed on the centralization of authority, not on factors that promote teamwork and organizational flexibility. That kind of approach does not reflect the preferences of Latin American culture.

Teamwork, subcontracting and geographical mobility

According to the study, Latin American culture "tends to favor the development of teamwork". Employees value social relationships based on personal communication and empathy, concepts that are essential to teamwork. Nevertheless, it is not easy to make this work, because power sharing and decentralization run against the grain of such Latin American cultural values as centralization and organizational hierarchy.

The hybrid model of management is clear when it comes to working arrangements. Although employees accept the idea of getting involved in modern managerial practices, they prefer a managerial style in which one senior executive makes the decisions. This frees each employee from taking responsibility. Executives who have higher education are the exception to this rule, however. Sharing responsibility for decision-making has other advantages. It allows companies to resolve conflicts and confrontations. Latin Americans traditionally accept the sort of manager who acts as a mediator between parties in a conflict. "That style may well be necessary, given the dynamics involved when working in groups," says the study.

Workers feel motivated to share the responsibilities of their team. However, as the authors note, this can also provide "another way for people to cut their individual risk by sharing decision-making with other individuals in the company".

The authors warn that modern approaches to organizing work may wind up failing in Latin America because of historic rivalries between management and labor during the region's industrialization process. Sometimes, managers have been accused of exploiting workers. However, this situation changes radically when there is a threat coming from outside and, for example, foreign investment threatens local employment. Whenever that happens, Latin America's sense of nationalism surges, along with its sense of unity that provokes "the desire to manufacture higher-quality products and use technology more efficiently", says the study. "Both those goals force senior management to learn how to share information with employees."

Latin America could benefit from any cut in labor costs that might result from creating more flexible labor contracts. However, it will be hard to convince workers to accept those sorts of conditions. Although many workers have only one option when they go looking for work, the most highly valued employees are, logically, those who work full-time. They receive benefits and promotional opportunities not provided to part-time employees.

The lack of geographical mobility is another challenge for both executives and employees. Some Latin American executives push for their companies to expand beyond borders, and they take responsible positions outside their homelands. However, most executives prefer to stay close to their nuclear families. In an interview, a senior executive of Coca Cola América Latina explained, "Because of personality and culture, Latin Americans generally lack the flexibility they need. In the United States, families get together only once a year, at Thanksgiving. In Mexico and Brazil, families see each other every Sunday."

Communication within a typical Latin American organization has a hierarchical and vertical structure in which "information generally flows from above, down to the bottom", says the study. Managers impose those barriers. Add the fact that subordinates lack a spirit of confrontation, and it's no wonder that communications are less than adequate. There are fewer horizontal relationships, and authority is rarely delegated.

Their own styles of confrontation

Establishing solid, stable labor relations requires personal contacts as well as friendly, social interaction. According to the study, "courtesy and diplomacy are highly valued in labor relations". Each Latin American country has its own confrontational style in times of conflict. "For example, Argentines prefer a style that involves mediating between parties in a conflict. Dominicans prefer autocratic intermediaries. Mexicans like a style that involves concern for others." Beyond that, "during times of conflict, Latin Americans tend to identify with their 'in-group', rather than the entire organization, because they prefer social networks based on friendship".

When multinational managers behave abusively, workers immediately organize unions and confront the company.

In conclusion, the authors make the following proposals: From a social perspective, they recommend putting workers and their families at the center of any additional benefits that the company provides. They also recommend that the Human Resource staff try to satisfy workers' basic needs, to assure their success. Finally, they argue that HR systems will become more effective if they support job stability, stronger labor-management relations, and the sustainable development of the company.

They warn, however, that "Human Resource departments will not be able to achieve a strategic position in the companies of the region until they demonstrate their direct contribution to overall organizational performance". The performance of HR departments must be viewed from a cultural perspective. Their challenge is to learn how to use culturally determined Human Resource practices — whose manifestations are hard to predict — and base them more on the organization's social structure than on its economics.

UNIT 5

Oil-producing Countries in North America and Northern Europe

Overview

North America is a continent that includes Canada, the United States, Mexico, Central America and the islands of the Caribbean Sea. In general, it is defined as any country to the north of (and including) Panama. Because countries south of the United States are usually called Latin American countries, in this Chapter, we only refer to North America as the area north of Mexico. Canada and United States are two of the largest countries in the world. They are friendly neighbor states and share a large border. Ninety percent of Canada's residents live within 100 miles of the United States border, so it is a reasonable conclusion that the two countries share many cultural similarities. However, the two nations show a difference between them in terms of several aspects such as climate, population, transport system, places of tourist interest, government and the like.

Although the definitions of the extent of Northern Europe vary, as per the United Nations geoscheme for Europe, Northern Europe comprises of 10 sovereign nations. Among them Norway has significant oil deposits, and is one of the world's largest exporters of natural gas.

Task 1 Topic discussion.

Can you list some keywords to describe North America and Northern Europe?

North America: ______________________________

____

____

Northern Europe: ____

____

____

Task 2 Watch the video and then fill in the blanks.[①]

In the world, there are unique places, rich in culture, unspoiled nature, and congenial to travelers. Welcome to Canada, one of the world's 1__________ countries.

It is a culturally diverse nation, with people of 2__________ being predominant. Canada has a population of about 3__________, over 4__________ of which live in the country's three largest cities: Montreal, Toronto, and Vancouver.

Canada's sophisticated cordial cities are national treasures with major attractions. Every one of Canada's 5__________ has something special to offer visitors, from wild life tours and fishing in the north, to kayak and nature tours in the Maritimes, from 6__________ in British Columbia, to enjoying the resorts and culture of Québec, from canoeing and 7__________ in Ontario, to 8__________ unique areas and museums on the prairie. The variety of the scenic beauty is absolutely 9__________.

The Horseshoe Falls or Niagara Falls Ontario is one of the world's most impressive and voluminous waterfalls. The Canadian Rockies is a vast, protected wildness area with 10__________ recreational and scenic attractions. Canada is a country with many blessings.

Task 3 Watch the video about the differences between America and Canada and list the 10 differences mentioned.[②]

1. ______________________ 2. ______________________

3. ______________________ 4. ______________________

5. ______________________ 6. ______________________

7. ______________________ 8. ______________________

9. ______________________ 10. ______________________

---

① The video can be accessed here: https://v.youku.com/v_show/id_XNDQ0NzE1NjQzMg==.html.

② The video can be accessed here: https://www.bilibili.com/video/BV1ox411U7sf/?spm_id_from=333.788.recommend_more_video.2.

Task 4 Watch the video about Norway and answer the following questions.[1]

1. Where is Norway located?

____

____

2. According to the free roaming law, what can people do in Norway?

____

____

3. What is the national dish of Norway?

____

____

Task 5 Understand Canada through film.

Bon Cop Bad Cop is a 2006 Canadian dark comedy-thriller buddy cop film about two police officers. The film has the distinctive feature of being bilingual, and it plays the linguistic and cultural differences between Québec and other parts of Canada to advantage. The characters of two detectives, David Bouchard from Québec and Martin Ward from Toronto, exaggerate and vividly portray these differences to the great delight of audiences.

Discuss the differences between the two cops with examples.

____

____

____

____

____

① The video can be accessed here: https://www.bilibili.com/video/BV19f4y1y7cC?spm_id_from=333.337.search-card.all.click.

Lead in

America, Canada and Norway are among the major oil-producing countries in the world. Search for information about oil production of the three countries in the most recent year.

Country	Rank	Production	Top oil and gas companies
USA			
Canada			
Norway			

Text A

Canadian Icons and Emblems[①]

Every country has a set of patriotic icons that citizens use to celebrate the uniqueness of their homeland, and Canada is no exception. Canada's national emblems run the gamut from historic and dignified to modern and corny, but rare is the Canadian who doesn't feel at least a little twinge of pride towards them.

The maple leaf

The distinctively-shaped maple leaf is the most common catch-all symbol for Canada, appearing not only on the Canadian national flag, but virtually every logo of a Canadian corporation or charity, or any other organization that needs to make its "Canadianness" instantly known.

The maple leaf is a symbol that's been so famous for so long that no one seems to remember exactly where it came from or how it got to be so popular. Various species of maple trees can be found in most regions of Canada, and their multipurpose functionality as both a provider of lumber and edible, sweet syrup has proved useful to many generations of Canadians over the centuries. In one sense, the maple can be viewed as a tree that rewards labour and perseverance, and evokes the history of early Canadians able to "tame" the wilderness for their own benefit. But to many others, it's simply a pretty tree with a pretty leaf that has become associated with Canada — and that's good enough.

① Canadian Icons and Emblems. (2016-11-17) [2022-04-14]. https://thecanadaguide.com/symbols/emblems/.

The Canadian flag

Like every other country on earth, Canada has a national flag suitable for flying, hanging or waving in any circumstance where a bit of patriotic pride is needed. Adopted in 1965, the official flag of Canada is known as the Maple Leaf, and consists of a stylized red leaf on a white background bordered by two red bars on either side. Unusually for a national flag, no part of the design is supposed to represent anything in particular; the stylized leaf was simply created as a neutral symbol of Canadian unity, and there is no official explanation of what the colours or bars are supposed to mean.

Canadian animals

The wilderness itself may be Canada's most iconic symbol. As an enormous country with more untouched nature than any other, it's unsurprising a vast assortment of things associated with the great outdoors feature so prominently in the Canadian gallery of national symbols. As the original residents of nature, Canada's diverse array of wild animals are among its most famous representatives.

The beaver is the most famous Canadian animal. It appears on the Canadian nickel and is often used by cartoonists to personify the country as a whole, much like "Uncle Sam" or a Chinese dragon. Though today beavers are often celebrated for their plucky, hardworking character, chomping down trees to build elaborate live-in dams, the original Canadian attraction to beavers was much less respectful: They had good fur for making hats. Prized for its smooth, waterproof texture, beaver fur was one of Canada's main exports to Europe during the 17th and 18th centuries. In fact, the animal was almost hunted to extinction by early Canadian fur traders. Saved by changing tastes in fashion, today they can be found lurking in riverbeds all across the country.

Less rich in specific symbolism are some of the beaver's furry pals, such as the moose, the polar bear, the black bear, the mountain lion, the mountain goat, the elk, the Arctic wolf, the raccoon, the lynx and the bison, all of which are common sights not only in the Canadian wilderness, but also Canadian airport gift shops. And then there are the birds, including the loon — the national bird of Canada and namesake of the loonie — and the not-quite-so beloved Canada goose, an elegant-looking animal that is nevertheless quite ornery and unpleasant in its interactions with humans. Every province has its own official bird as well, the most famous of which are probably the snowy owl of Québec and the puffin of Prince Edward Island.

The Canadian Coat of Arms

Like most countries of European heritage, Canada has a grandiose heraldic symbol known as the Coat of Arms (also known as the national crest) that appears on things like passports, government publications and wax seals. It's a very complicated and detailed illustration that is almost entirely identical to Britain's Royal Coat of Arms, which dates back to the 17th century.

The crest's symbolism is largely British: It depicts an English lion and a Scottish unicorn holding a shield displaying medieval icons of the English, Scottish, and Irish peoples of the British Isles, plus the fleur-de-lis of the French and the maple leaves of Canada. At the creatures' feet sit a medley of plants representing the Scottish, Irish, English, and Welsh. The animals stand below the flags of the United Kingdom and medieval France, symbolizing the "two founding nations" of modern Canada.

Canada has two national mottoes, both of which are inscribed in Latin on the crest. The first (on the red belt around the shield) is Desiderantes Meliorem Patriam, or "They Desire a Better Country", which acknowledges the immigrants who have built Canada and Canadians' ongoing desire for national self-improvement. The other (on the blue ribbon at the bottom) is A Mari usque ad Mare, or "From Sea to Sea".

Mounties

Officers of the Royal Canadian Mounted Police (RCMP), nicknamed Mounties, have been one of Canada's most iconic symbols for generations.

The RCMP was founded in 1873, originally known as the North-West Mounted Police, and was initially used to bring law and order to Canada's newly-acquired Prairie provinces and northern territories. Their adventures in the untamed Canadian wilderness, full of wild animals, crazy cowboys, greedy prospectors, and (as they saw it) dangerous Indians became the subject of many Hollywood movies in the early 20th century, and helped make Canada's cops an internally-known symbol of Canadian life.

Today, RCMP officers rarely wear their iconic red uniforms and wide-brimmed hats except on ceremonial occasions, but full-dressed officers are a common sight on Canadian souvenirs, postcards, and toys.

The national anthem

There have been a lot of patriotic songs written about Canada over the years, but until 1980 none held the lofty status of Canada's official national anthem. Initially, the country was just supposed to use *God Save the Queen*, the royal anthem of Great Britain, for official purposes, but as the years went on there was growing interest in using a more uniquely Canadian song, with *The Maple Leaf Forever* (1867) and *O Canada* (1880) emerging as the two most popular tunes. *O Canada* eventually won out, and was given official anthem status when Parliament passed the National Anthem Act in 1980.

Exercises

Task 1 Match the words with their explanations.

patriotic	an iconic image or thing is important or impressive because it seems to be a symbol of something
perseverance	to write or cut words, your name, etc. onto sth.
evoke	to show an image of sb./sth. in a picture
neutral	having or expressing a great love of your country
iconic	to bring a feeling, a memory or an image into your mind
assortment	that does not let water through or that cannot be damaged by water
elaborate	very complicated and detailed; carefully prepared and organized
waterproof	the quality of continuing to try to achieve a particular aim despite difficulties
depict	a collection of different things or of different types of the same thing
inscribe	not supporting or helping either side in a disagreement, competition, etc.

Task 2 Answer the following questions according to the information from text A.

1. What can maple trees be used for?

____

____

2. What were the beavers originally used for?

____

____

3. List the elements of Canadian Coat of Arms.

____

____

4. What was RCMP initially used to do?

____

____

5. Which song is Canada's national anthem?

____

____

Task 3 Translate the following sentences into Chinese.

1. In one sense, the maple can be viewed as a tree that rewards labour and perseverance, and evokes the history of early Canadians able to "tame" the wilderness for their own benefit.

____

____

2. In fact, the animal was almost hunted to extinction by early Canadian fur traders. Saved by changing tastes in fashion, today they can be found lurking in riverbeds all across the country.

____

____

3. Their adventures in the untamed Canadian wilderness, full of wild animals, crazy cowboys, greedy prospectors, and (as they saw it) dangerous Indians became the subject of many Hollywood movies in the early 20th century, and helped make Canada's cops an internally-known symbol of Canadian life.

____

____

Task 4 Critical thinking enhancement.

In Canada, there has been debate over the beaver's merits as a symbol. Read the following statements and decide whether they agree or disagree with using beaver as a symbol of Canada and summarize the reasons.

1. "I'm a big fan of the symbol of the beaver because I feel a country gets the animal it deserves. A beaver is an unaggressive, hard-working, waterproof, unassuming, wonderful animal and I think it speaks well of Canadians that we chose it. And even if the fur trade is long dead and in the ground, I think it still works."
2. "Historically, the beaver has a lot of connections with Canada, but unfortunately the rest of the world doesn't know about the history. And even if they did know, the beaver's history

was to be stripped bare and sold to foreigners, which you could argue from an economic standpoint is not an entirely inaccurate depiction of Canadian history."

3. "I guess you could argue the beaver is industrious — busy as a beaver is the phrase — but is that accurate to describe Canadians as busy people? I don't really think it fits."
4. "England has the lion, Russia has the bear, France has the rooster. Whereas our humble beaver is much more egalitarian...We're not grand. We're the hard-working good guys."

Text B

Why Is Norway So Good at the Winter Games?[①]

There's a familiar country atop the medal count in the Winter Olympics: Norway. The country has even set a new mark for most gold medals in a single Winter Games with 16 in Beijing. This might surprise some given that Norway has only a little more than five million residents — not even in the top 100 most populated countries. Norway is the birthplace of skiing but that was millennia ago and they haven't rested on their laurels. It's also a great destination to have a go at a huge range of other winter sports.

Norwegians are reluctant to brag (they prefer to do things quietly, including becoming the wealthiest country in the world). But all the evidence suggests they invented skiing. The word itself comes from the Norse word for planks, skíð, while Neolithic carvings from 5000 BCE depict skiers.

While other Alpine nations were on the nursery slopes, Norway was scoring many firsts in winter sports: the first ski jumper (a soldier called Olaf Rye Telemark, 1809); the first ski competition (Tromsø, 1843); the first ski clubs (Trysil, 1861). And it's not just ancient history. As well as winning the most Winter Olympics medals, Norway, topped the table once again in 2022.

So what's the secret to Norway's historical and current success? There are two big factors.

The first is, perhaps obviously, the weather. It's the Winter Olympics after all. Norway ranks in the bottom five for average temperature during the year at about 36 degrees Fahrenheit (two degrees Celsius).

But it's more than temperature. It is also money.

Think about how hard it is to train for the Olympics. Gear is often expensive. Children often need fortunate enough parents to get them to events. There also needs to be infrastructure in place to train for the Olympics.

Norway is a fairly wealthy country: Its GDP is in the top 35 worldwide and the GDP per capita is in the top 10. GDP though doesn't capture all types of wealth. That's what the United Nations Inequality-adjusted Human Development Index is for; it takes into account other variables such as education, life expectancy and inequality.

Vetle Sjåstad Christiansen, who won gold in the men's 4×7.5 km biathlon relay and

---

① ENTEN H. Why Is Norway So Good at the Winter Games? (2022-02-18) [2022-04-14]. https://edition.cnn.com/2022/02/18/sport/why-norway-is-so-good-winter-olympics-beijing-2022-spt-intl/index.html. BRITTON B. The Secret Behind Norway's Winter Olympic Success. (2018-02-25) [2022-04-14]. https://edition.cnn.com/2018/02/24/sport/norway-winter-olympic-success-intl/index.html.

bronze in 15 km mass start, outlined some of the expensive technology and techniques he and his teammates used to cope with the testing conditions in China.

"For the biathlon team, it's been an unbelievable journey this Olympics in Beijing. We were a little bit afraid that maybe here with the wind and the cold it would be some surprises and a little bit of coincidences. So the last two, three years we tried to eliminate as much of these coincidences as we possibly could like training a lot in the altitude, training a lot in the wind. When we didn't have real wind, we trained with wind machine and put it behind us to have some wind from the left because we knew here from the data that it would be a lot of wind from the left. It's very good to see that we get value for the work we have done the last two and a half years."

A country where knowledge can be transferred and where more of the country has access to the funds necessary to compete would in theory supply a broader array of athletes. You know where Norway is on the Inequality-adjusted Human Development Index? Number one. It shouldn't be too surprising, therefore, that a wealthy country — where it is also cold — dominates the Winter Games.

Despite being the current leader in Winter Olympic medals, there have been times when Norway suffered dismal results — notably at the Calgary 1988 Winter Olympics. Here, it failed to win even one gold.

That's when Norway's sporting body restructured and before hosting the Winter Games in Lillehammer in 1994, it established a national elite sports center — the Olympiatoppen — to train and develop Norway's best athletes.

"When there was a crisis something had to happen," Tore Øvrebø, Norway's Olympic chief, former Olympic rower, explained. "The sporting systems in the rest of the world were more and more professionalized and we didn't do the same in Norway."

He said there was a huge change after the center was set up.

"It was a new way of thinking for sports. (Federation) presidents were not that important anymore and we wanted to have professional people working directly with high performance."

Since 1994, the establishment of Olympiatoppen has overseen 20 years of significant improvement — most particularly in cross-country skiing. Funding for the Olympiatoppen has also increased exponentially. In 1990, it had a budget of $2.4 million — with 73 percent of its expenditure going towards support for athletes and teams. By 2001, the budget had increased to $12.3 million and now it's over $24.2 million.

While funding helps, Øvrebø also said Norway's high standard of living also plays a part in creating world-class athletes, notably in offering free healthcare and education. According to the World Economic Forum, Norway "is a star performer across almost every one of the OECD's indicators both for material conditions and quality of life".

"That makes people quite well off at the beginning," added Øvrebø. "It means they can follow their interests. It's a very humanistic approach."

As a result, he said, "Many kids are choosing to play the sport. That means we can recruit athletes from quite high — we have all these people doing the sport and the possibility to do it because they're healthy and are being taken care of."

Exercises

Task 1 Use the proper forms of the words in the table to complete the following sentences. You may not use any of the words in the table more than once.

infrastructure	altitude	exponentially	oversee	reluctant
coincidence	gear	millennium	nursery	expectancy

1. The former head of the UNESCO World Heritage Centre, which __________ heritage sites, is Francesco Bandarin, a Venetian who now serves as UNESCO's assistant director-general for culture.
2. By __________, I met the person we'd been discussing the next day.
3. Not like others, he chose to stay in front of his computer to welcome the New __________.
4. Snow leopards live at high __________.
5. The government has been extremely __________ to expedite investigations that might result in his trial.
6. The survey shows that people now have a higher life __________.
7. The __________, from hotels to transport, is old and decrepit.
8. An affordable __________ education service is an essential basic amenity.
9. The quantity of chemical pollutants has increased __________.
10. About 100 officers in riot __________ were needed to break up the fight.

Task 2 Answer the following questions according to the information from text B.

1. What are the two factors for Norway's success in winter sport?

____

____

2. What did Norway team do to deal with the surprises and coincidences resulting from the cold and wind in Beijing?

____

____

3. What did Norway do after suffering dismal results in 1988 Winter Olympic Games?

____

____

Task 3 Translate the following sentences into Chinese.

1. While other Alpine nations were on the nursery slopes, Norway was scoring many firsts in winter sports: the first ski jumper (a soldier called Olaf Rye Telemark, 1809); the first ski competition (Tromsø, 1843); the first ski clubs (Trysil, 1861).

____

____

2. A country where knowledge can be transferred and where more of the country has access to the funds necessary to compete would in theory supply a broader array of athletes.

____

____

3. Despite being the current leader in Winter Olympic medals, there have been times when Norway suffered dismal results — notably at the Calgary 1988 Winter Olympics.

____

____

Task 4 Please write an essay of 300 words to discuss the following issue.

Gender equality is a fundamental human right and achieving equality between women and men is embedded in the UN Sustainable Development Goals (SDG). Norway is considered to be one of the most gender equal countries in the world. Discuss how gender equality is achieved in Norway.

____

____

____

____

____

Text C

Oil Production of Canada and America

Canada: oil sands①

The Canadian oil sands (or tar sands) are a large area of petroleum extraction from bitumen, located primarily along the Athabasca River with its centre of activity close to Fort McMurray in Alberta, approximately 400 km northeast of the provincial capital, Edmonton. Increased global energy demand, high petroleum dependency and geopolitical conflict in key oil-producing regions have driven the exploration of unconventional oil sources since the 1970s which, paired with advances in the field of petroleum engineering, has continued to make bitumen extraction economically profitable at a time of rising oil prices.

Alberta's first commercial oil sands operation started in 1967. The exploration of oil sands significantly increased Canada's total oil reserves from approximately five billion barrels to an estimated 173 billion, meaning Canada has the third largest oil reserve in the world, with 97 percent of the oil in the form of oil sands. The sands cover about 140,000 km^2. About 66 percent of them have already been leased to companies for oil sands extraction. In 2012, oil sands extraction contributed an estimated $91 billion to Canada's gross domestic product, and over 475,000 jobs (three percent of the nation's total) may have benefited to some extent. Over half of Canada's oil production currently comes from the oil sands (about 1.8 million out of 3.2 million barrels per day). Growth trajectories vary, but production may double in volume between 2010 and 2030 to 6.7 million barrels per day, with all growth coming from the oil sands.

Oil sands extraction occurs through two major approaches: surface mining and deep drilling called in situ. Surface mining first strips the area of the so-called overburden (i.e., vegetation, soil and earth layers above the bitumen), and creates large open-pit mines from which the bitumen is removed with shovels and trucks to be physically and chemically processed. Based on current technologies and their economic costs, oil sands operators use surface mining for areas where the bitumen is up to 70–100 m below the surface. For areas where the bitumen layer is deeper, in situ drilling is used. As the Latin term for "on site" suggests, this type of drilling leaves the vegetation and soil layers above the bitumen largely

① DAVIDSEN C. Oil Sands. (2018-02-03) [2022-04-15]. https://www.thecanadianencyclopedia.ca/en/article/oil-sands.

intact and instead pressure-pumps the bitumen to the surface after heating it underground. The technologies that made this method possible — steam-assisted gravity drainage (SAGD) and cyclic steam stimulation (CSS) — marked the beginning of large-scale commercial in situ drilling, which significantly changed the dimensions of Canadian oil sands extraction from the early 2000s on.

Environmental impacts and concerns from oil sands extraction are multifold and affect the region as well as the planet. They include high carbon and other greenhouse gas emissions; regional air pollution; introducing toxic materials in the soil, water and air; loss of ecological habitat and biodiversity; water pollution; forest destruction; toxicity and seepage from tailings ponds; ecological restoration prospects after mining impacts; and high input of energy and water in general. Surface mining in particular has come under public scrutiny for its visible ecological impacts on the natural landscape. Over 715 km^2 of boreal forest have already been destroyed or affected by oil sands mining and an additional 4,700 km^2 have been licensed for surface mining (an area roughly 78 times the size of New York City's Manhattan Island). To produce one barrel of oil from surface mining, up to two tonnes of tar sands must be moved depending on the location, two to five barrels of water used and an estimated 35 kg of carbon dioxide are emitted. In situ drilling leaves the vegetation cover of the immediate extraction area intact, but it widens the geographic reach of oil sands extraction significantly into areas where the bitumen layers are too deep to be viable for surface mining. It has high environmental costs, too; every barrel of oil produced by steam-assisted gravity drilling causes an estimated 55 kg of carbon emissions and burns 28 m^3 of natural gas. Over 88,000 km^2 have been licensed for in situ drilling as of January 2013.

The environmental and social impacts of the Canadian oil sands have led to widespread debate and critiques over the scope of their future development. There are ongoing discussions about environmental regulations and ecological monitoring practices, decision-making and approval processes, distribution of economic benefits between Canadian taxpayers and foreign investors, as well as socio-economic benefits for the region. Canada and Alberta's carbon and energy strategies have also been called into question, as have the energy input and emission levels for the oil sands. For many, the subject underlying all of these debates is the global rise of energy consumption and demand, which has opened debates on ecological modernization and an energy transition to shift society away from petroleum dependency.

America: three reasons why the US is now the world's largest oil producer[①]

The US is the world's largest oil producer, thanks to a decline in production costs and

① Three Reasons Why the US Is Now the World's Largest Oil Producer. (2022-01-31) [2022-04-15]. https://www.offshore-technology.com/comment/three-reasons-us-now-worlds-largest-oil-producer/.

faltering competitors. It overtook Russia during June and August 2018, and had already surpassed Saudi Arabia earlier in the year. Booming shale oil production enabled the domestic industry to reach 10 million bpd this year for the first time since the 1970s. For the remainder of 2018 and for at least 2019, US supply is predicted to maintain the number one slot according to the EIA. Yet the impact the government and US-based oil majors can have on the international market is likely to carry on getting bigger.

Even though production growth is predicted to slow, the US will account for over half of worldwide expansion in the next five years according to IEA. The key reasons behind this include Saudi Arabia's cuts, the US being outside OPEC, and cost efficiencies in drilling.

Assuming the top spot demonstrates the influence of the world's largest economy on oil, the rising expense of Saudi Arabia is having a direct impact. Reports suggest that Saudi Arabia was seeking investment from the Russian Direct Investment Fund, Russia's sovereign wealth fund, in the initial public offering (IPO) of Aramco, the Saudi state oil producer. This highlights the Kingdom's uncertainty regarding its future in oil. Under such circumstances, rising US oil flows exacerbates the gains in influence on the global oil industry the country has gained in the recent past. Saudi Arabia trimming production during July helped enhance the influence of the US on global oil supplies.

Not in the bounds of OPEC, US oil firms are free to choose to what extent capacity growth is pursued, eroding the influence of other oil producing states. The US is also relatively stable, while several significant OPEC producers face chronic instability. While oil producing states such as Venezuela and Iran saw production decline, OPEC levels were boosted by Saudi Arabia and Nigeria in August 2018. Iraq and Libya both increased production levels, but Iraq is experiencing civil unrest around Basra where its oil production facilities are, and Libya remains chronically unstable. Iran faces US sanctions virtually destroying its exports, while Venezuela also faces an economic crisis which has led to a collapse in production.

Oil majors operating in the US have achieved the expansion thanks to far improved cost efficiency drilling in the Gulf of Mexico. Conventional wisdom dictates conditions in the Arabian oil nations are somewhat easier and cheaper than those to be found in the Gulf of Mexico. Yet costs, however, have come down substantially, allowing oil from the Gulf to be drilled at much more competitive prices. Gone are the "gold plated" bespoke rigs. Oil majors are sharing rig designs between oil fields, adapting them to suit local conditions.

Exercises

Task 1 Answer the following questions according to the information from text C.

1. What are the major extraction methods of oil sands?

____

____

2. What are the environmental impacts of oil sand extraction?

____

____

3. Briefly explain the reasons why America is now the largest oil producer.

____

____

Task 2 Translate the following sentences into Chinese.

1. The Canadian oil sands (or tar sands) are a large area of petroleum extraction from bitumen, located primarily along the Athabasca River with its centre of activity close to Fort McMurray in Alberta, approximately 400 km northeast of the provincial capital, Edmonton.

____

____

2. Surface mining first strips the area of the so-called overburden (i.e., vegetation, soil and earth layers above the bitumen), and creates large open-pit mines from which the bitumen is removed with shovels and trucks to be physically and chemically processed.

____

____

3. Assuming the top spot demonstrates the influence of the world's largest economy on oil, the rising expense of Saudi Arabia is having a direct impact.

____

____

Task 3 Critical thinking enhancement.

What do you think of the future development of Canada's oil industry? Do you think America will maintain its first position in oil production in the long run?

____

____

____

____

____

Practical Tips

The Social Do's and Don'ts of Norwegian Society①

Every child grows up raised on a set of social rules. In the U.S.A. you always say your "please and thank you". In Nepal, you always accept a meal and a steaming mug of Chai tea when offered. In Japan, you always respect the elderly and obey your parents. In Norway, they have their own sets of social rules every Norwegian has been raised on.

Best for everyone

With a population of 5 million people, and a country rich in resources, Norwegians have set up their country to support its citizens, take care of its people, and create equal life quality for everyone. Ingrained in this foundation is an overall cultural norm of equality, commonality and respect. Even in the work place, the boss is the boss, but Norwegian work culture has much more of a flat hierarchical structure than other countries. As a person functioning in Norwegian society, one individual does not deserve more than another, and Norwegians view the entire systems functionality with more importance than that of one person.

Do I know you?

As a visitor to Norway, you will likely encounter friendly and helpful locals as you travel the country. A genuine interest in outsiders and a deep pride for their country follows Norwegians nationally, and they want to share it with you. English is commonly spoken, although in some smaller towns you may have to search a little bit to find someone fluent. However, in the daily life, Norwegians do not often socialize with those they don't know. Being self-sufficient, not bothering others, and being quiet are common Norwegian social norms in the daily life. However, things change when you're in the mountains. The second Norwegians put on their hiking boots and take to the mountains, you can greet and chat with anyone you like.

Competition? I'm in

Competitive games or sports are highly valued in Norway. Whether it's your intellect, athleticism, or a simple game of cards, Norwegians thrive on competition. Turning anything into a game where one can win will often make you a crowd-pleaser in any Norwegian setting.

---

① SMITH A. The Social Do's and Don'ts of Norwegian Society. (2019-10-29) [2022-04-16]. https://hvitserk.norrona.com/en/resources/tips-and-tricks/the-social-dos-and-donts-of-norwegian-society?msclkid=493238beba3411ecbf53758b07ab15e2.

However, if you do win, the right to brag or be proud of your success does not come with the territory.

Nature in any weather

Most Norwegians grow up with access to nature, and the society as a whole values time spent outside with your family. This connection to nature can be observed in their large cities — often with public transport access to limitless forest trails; their fashion-tennis shoes with your business skirt is 100% acceptable and rain jackets are very in; on Sundays most stores are closed and the day is to be spent with your family picking berries, walking the trails, or enjoying a swim. Even our candy bars. Have you heard of Kvikk Lunsj? This best-selling hiking candy bar has a set of mountain rules written on its wrapper, thus reminding candy eaters everywhere how to stay safe in the mountains.

All in all, the Norwegian phrases "There is no bad weather, only bad clothing" or "Nature, it's in our blood" generalize the common tough Norwegian mentality towards being outside. Norway's weather systems can be adverse, and Norwegians take that challenge head on and embrace it. Want to go outside? Then bundle up, no complaints, and off we go!

Follow the rules

With this highly functional society comes the expectation that you will follow the rules, even if they are not enforced. Looking for loopholes in the system or bending the rulebook is just not a concept in Norway. Every Norwegian respects the rule book, whether social norms, cultural expectations, tradition, or the laws and regulations from the government. If there is a rule, there is a reason, so trust the system and do as you're told. That is the best outcome for the whole, and everybody matters.

The Norwegian Arm

Have you had the experience of your grandmother shaming you for reaching across the dinner table to grab some salt? Some potatoes? Maybe some butter? That's rude, we learn. Well, you can let go of those years of training and polite "Could you please pass me the salt". In Norway, use of the "Norwegian Arm" is a given at any sit-down meal. Need something across the table? Go ahead and just grab it, even if your arm crosses someone else's personal space. It's okay! Really. Embrace the Norwegian Arm mentality and reach for whatever you need!

Excuse me, here is a cheese slicer

Do you love cheese? Well, Norwegians do too, but they handle their cheese needs a bit differently than other countries. If you're used to taking out a kitchen or pocket knife to chop off a chunk of cheese, think again. You're in Norway now. The idea of hacking away at a lovely symmetrical block of cheese with a knife is mildly unthinkable. They invented cheese slicers. Use them! Slice nice and thin slices of cheese off, place them on your meal, and leave the block of cheese nice and clean for the next user. This is necessary with any kind of cheese, including brown cheese, a Norwegian sweet cheese you have to try if visiting Norway. Our suggestion? One slice of brown cheese with a little bit of jam on Knekkebrød (seed-cracker bread), and voila! Enjoy.

Want a drink? Bring your own

Alcohol is expensive in Norway. It is heavily taxed and can be somewhat challenging to come by if you're not at the right place at the right time. Beer and drinks under 4.75% alcohol are sold in common grocery stores until 8 pm on weekdays, or 6 pm on Saturdays, and there is no alcohol for sale on Sundays (Mostly everything else is closed on Sundays as well). Anything with a higher alcohol level is sold at the Wine Monopoly. Yes, you heard me right, Monopoly. There is only one store in Norway that sells alcohol above 4.75%, and they close at 3 pm on Saturdays. Purchasing a drink out on the town will cost you between 12$ USD and 25$ USD. Conclusion? Plan ahead for your weekends, and keep an eye on your watch. A spur of the moment beer run is not so easily done in Norway, and if you are going to a local's house for dinner, the ultimate gesture of hospitality would be to bring some drinks to share with you. However, in Norway, this is not expected, or even common… maybe even a little weird. Those meeting to enjoy a meal together don't expect either the host or guest to supply alcoholic beverages — drinks with dinner are an individual affair, so if you're going to a gathering, bring your own drinks.

17th of May

If you're traveling to Norway on May 17th, make sure you join the celebrations. Norway's National Day is an experience you are sure to remember. Men, women and children dress up in their national costume — the Bunad — and take to the streets to party, play games, parade with Norwegian flags, and eat Kransekake (cake) with tiny Norwegian flags decorating the dessert. Not only will you consume mass amounts of Kransekake, but also look forward to the ice cream competitions all Norwegians take part in. How many ice creams did you eat on 17th of May this year? Follow this delicious tradition up with as many hot dogs as possible and you have the complete image of Norway's National Day.

Ski event? Norwegians will all be there

When the 1994 Olympics came to Norway, thousands of Norwegians camped out in the forest in −20 degree weather... just waiting for a glimpse of their national athletes to ski by their camp. Cross country ski racing, ski jumping and biathlons are three of Norway's national sports, and the dedicated fans will go above and beyond to support them. If you have the opportunity to join a local ski event when traveling in Norway, take it! Nothing explains Norwegians better than observing them in their element... cheering on their nation's top athletes from the side lines.

A small gasp

Having a conversation with a Norwegian can leave one wondering if they're upset with you — they keep interrupting you and gasping. But have no fear, they're not. If a Norwegian is listening to you, it's common to hear a small intake of breath during conversation. This sounds somewhat like a small gasp. Again, it's okay, don't panic. They are just acknowledging you while you speak and breathing in sharply while they mutter a quiet "ja" (yes) to encourage you to continue.

Of course, we're generalizing

Not all Norwegians follow these social norms, but the overall culture embodied in the text above can give you some insight into the Norwegian culture. Should you happen upon masses of Norwegians cheering in their traditional Bunad, you can wonder if there is a ski competition nearby, or if traveling on May 17th, perhaps it is the Norway's National Day. These cultural norms can give you the extra boost of exploring another country and culture as you move through Norway's astounding natural landscape. Keep an eye out for these tell-tale Norwegian traditions, and enjoy your visit to this beautiful country.

UNIT 6

Oil-producing Countries in Southeast Asia

Overview

Southeast Asia or Southeastern Asia is a subregion of Asia, consisting of the countries that are geographically south of Japan, Korea and China, east of India, west of Papua New Guinea, and north of Australia. In contemporary definition, Southeast Asia consists of two geographic regions: Mainland Southeast Asia and Maritime Southeast Asia. The region lies near the intersection of geological plates, with both heavy seismic and volcanic activities.

The region is culturally and ethnically diverse, with hundreds of languages spoken by different ethnic groups. Ten countries in the region are members of the Association of Southeast Asian Nations (ASEAN), a regional organization established for economic, political, military, educational and cultural integration amongst its members.

Task 1 Topic discussion.

Southeast Asia is a collection of related but dissimilar states squeezed between the Indian Ocean and the Pacific Ocean. The area has long been a favorite corner of the world for globe-tramping backpackers, well-known for its perfect beaches, tasty cuisine, low prices, and good air connections. Suppose you are going to have a graduation trip in Southeast Asia, what places will be on your travel wish list and why?

____

____

____

____

____

Task 2 Listen to the following recording and then fill in the blanks.[①]

New research shows that factory activity across Southeast Asia fell sharply in July because of increasing cases of the coronavirus's Delta variant. The results were based on a series of 1__________ completed this week. The economic difficulties were also linked to slow progress in coronavirus vaccinations in many Southeast Asian nations.

Economic experts say the big drop in factory production threatens growth in some of the world's most resilient markets. Southeast Asia has survived several major economic crises in the past, partly because its nations have enacted 2__________ and the area is close to China. But the continuing coronavirus pandemic — driven by a recent rise in infections of the Delta variant — is creating new problems.

Economists with British-based banking group HSBC told Reuters news agency that low 3__________ in several countries are threatening these economies. They pointed to low vaccination rates in Vietnam, the Philippines and Thailand. "Populations in these countries could remain vulnerable not only to the current outbreak, but any 4__________ that may develop," HSBC said in a statement. "Virus-related restrictions are likely to continue," the bank said, "leaving many factories without workers."

Thailand is Asia's fourth-largest 5__________ and a production base for major world car brands. But Toyota suspended production in July at three of its factories in the country because of parts shortages caused by the pandemic. Siam Agro-Food Industry, a Thai processed fruit exporter, depends heavily on migrant labor. But it has only been able to fill 400 of 550 positions as workers return to their home countries and are not able to come back to work because of 6__________. The company's president, Ghanyapad Tantipipatpong, spoke to Reuters news agency. She said: "There are 350 tonnes of fruit per day, but now we can take only 250 tonnes because of not enough workers to process."

In Vietnam, several big international companies including Samsung, Foxconn and Nike, have production operations in the country. In the south, pandemic restrictions have forced some businesses to 7__________ at their production centers at night. Vietnam's government said last week that industrial production fell sharply in several southern cities facing restrictions since July.

Malaysia supplies about 67 percent of the worldwide rubber glove market. But pandemic restrictions forced 8__________ to halt production in June and July. An appeal by the country's glove-making association led to eased restrictions that permitted 60 percent of the workers to return. The association is now calling for a full return.

Factory slowdowns in Southeast Asia have already caused problems in other countries, including in Germany. German electronics maker Infineon Technologies said it is 9__________.

---

① The audio can be accessed here: https://www.21voa.com/VOA_Special_English/southeast-asia-factories-hurt-by-virus-and-vaccination-problems-23691.html.

The production problems will also affect Infineon's automotive customers, the company said. Daniel Bernbeck is head of the Malaysian–German Chamber of Commerce and Industry. He said Malaysia's current quarantine rules have made it difficult for manufacturers 10__________.

Task 3 Watch the TED talk titled *Life that doesn't end with death* and answer the following questions.①

Brief introduction to the speech: In Tana Toraja, weddings and births aren't the social gatherings that knit society together. In this part of Indonesia, big, raucous funerals are at the center of social life. The speaker takes a look at this culture, in which the bodies of dead relatives are cared for years after they have passed away — because relationships with loved ones don't simply end when breathing does.

1. Why is the funeral ceremony in Tana Toraja a raucous affair?

____

____

2. What can we gain from seeing physical death not only as a biological process but as part of the greater human story?

____

____

Task 4 Understand Southeast Asia through documentaries.②

The documentaries *Bridging Giants* tell stories between China and ASEAN countries. They lead the audience merging into a series of details of the lives of characters, and closely link the lives of ordinary people with the fruits of practical cooperation between China and ASEAN.

____

____

____

____

____

① The video can be accessed here: https://www.ted.com/talks/kelli_swazey_life_that_doesn_t_end_with_death.

② The videos can be accessed here: https://search.bilibili.com/all?keyword=Bridging%20Giants&from_source=webtop_search&spm_id_from=333.1007.

Lead in

The ASEAN is a regional intergovernmental organization comprising ten countries in Southeast Asia including Indonesia, Malaysia, Vietnam, Thailand, Brunei, Cambodia, Laos, Myanmar, Philippines and Singapore. ASEAN member countries are now among the most dynamic parts of the global energy system and a rising force in international energy affairs (see Figure 6-1) .

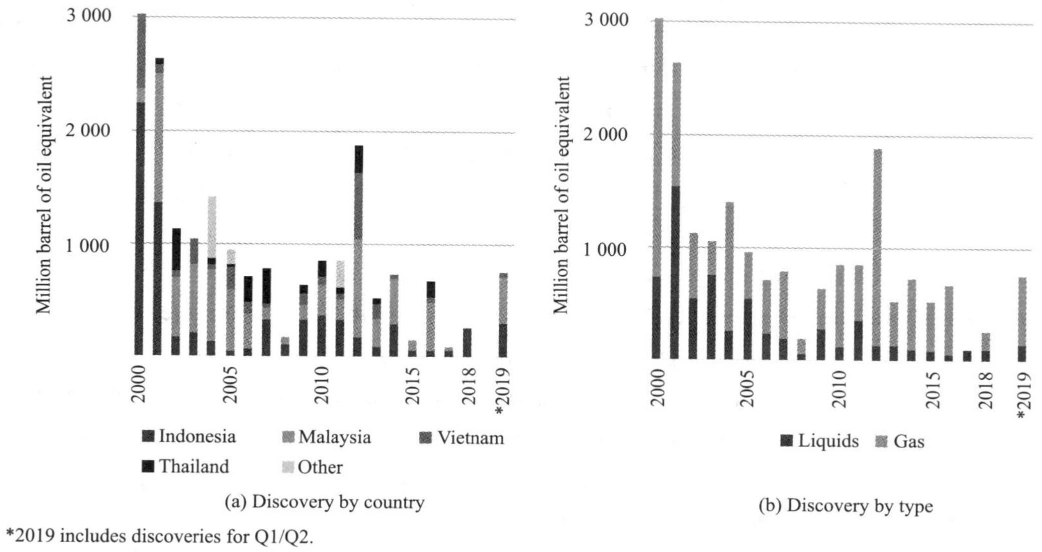

Figure 6-1 Oil and gas discoveries by country and type

(Source: IEA analysis based on Rystad Energy)

Text A

Approaching Indonesia①

The name Indonesia, meaning Indian Islands, was coined by an Englishman, J. R. Logan, in Malaya in 1850. Derived from the Greek, Indos (India) and nesos (island), it has parallels in Melanesia, "black islands"; Micronesia, "small islands"; and Polynesia, "many islands". A German geographer, Adolf Bastian, used it in the title of his book, *Indonesien*, in 1884, and in 1928 nationalists adopted it as the name of their hoped-for nation.

① Indonesia. [2022-04-24]. https://www.everyculture.com/Ge-It/Indonesia.html.

Indonesia, the world's largest archipelago nation, is located astride the equator in the humid tropics and extends some 2,300 miles east-west. It is surrounded by oceans, seas, and straits except where it shares an island border with East Malaysia and Brunei on Borneo (Kalimantan); with Papua New Guinea on New Guinea; and with Timor Loro Sae on Timor. West Malaysia lies across the Straits of Malaka, the Philippines lies to the northeast, and Australia lies to the south.

The archipelago's location has played a profound role in economic, political, cultural, and religious developments there. For more than two thousand years, trading ships sailed between the great civilizations of India and China via the waters and islands of the Indies. The islands also supplied spices and forest products to that trade. The alternating east and west monsoon winds made the Indies a layover point for traders and others from diverse nations who brought their languages, ideas about political order, and their arts and religions. Small and then large kingdoms grew as a result of, and as part of, that great trade. Steamships altered some trade patterns, but the region's strategic location between East and South Asia and the Middle East remains.

Indonesia consists of all or part of some of the world's largest islands — Sumatra, Java, most of Kalimantan (Borneo), Sulawesi (Celebes), Halmahera, and the west half of New Guinea (Papua) — and numerous smaller islands, of which Bali (just east of Java) is best known. There are some four hundred volcanoes on these islands, of which one hundred are active. Between 1973 and 1990, for example, there were twenty-nine recorded eruptions, some with tragic consequences. Volcanic lava and ash contributed to the rich soils of upland Sumatra and all of Java and Bali, which have nurtured rice cultivation for several thousand years.

Two types of agriculture are predominant in Indonesia: permanent irrigated rice farming (sawah) and rotating swidden or slash-and-burn (ladang) farming of rice, corn, and other crops. Many areas are rich in vegetables, tropical fruit, sago, and other cultivated or forest crops, and commercial plantations of coffee, tea, tobacco, coconuts, and sugar are found in both inner and outer islands. Plantation-grown products such as rubber, palm oil, and sisal are prominent in Sumatra, while coffee, sugar, and tea are prominent in Java. Maluku (formerly the Moluccas) gained its appellation the "Spice Islands" from the importance of trade. Gold, tin, and nickel are mined in Sumatra, Bangka, Kalimantan, Sulawesi, and Papua for domestic and international markets, and oil and liquefied natural gas (especially from Sumatra) are important exports. Numerous rivers flowing from mountainous or jungle interiors to coastal plains and ports have carried farm and forest products for centuries and have been channels for cultural communication.

Indonesian societies have a long history during which local and wider cultures were formed. About 200 C.E., small states that were deeply influenced by Indian civilization began to develop in Southeast Asia, primarily at estuaries of major rivers. The next five hundred to one thousand years saw great states arise with magnificent architecture. Hinduism and Buddhism, writing systems, notions of divine kingship, and legal systems from India were adapted to local scenes. Sanskrit terms entered many of the languages of Indonesia. Hinduism influenced cultures throughout Southeast Asia, but only one people are Hindu, the Balinese.

Indianized states declined about 1400 C.E. with the arrival of Muslim traders and teachers from India, Yemen, and Persia, and then Europeans from Portugal, Spain, Holland, and Britain. All came to join the great trade with India and China. Over the next two centuries local princedoms traded, allied, and fought with Europeans, and the Dutch East India Company became a small state engaging in local battles and alliances to secure trade. The Dutch East India Company was powerful until 1799 when the company went bankrupt. In the nineteenth century the Dutch formed the Netherlands Indies government, which developed alliances with rulers in the archipelago. Only at the beginning of the twentieth century did the Netherlands Indies government extend its authority by military means to all of present Indonesia.

Sporadic nineteenth century revolts against Dutch practices occurred mainly in Java, but it was in the early twentieth century that Indonesian intellectual and religious leaders began to seek national independence. In 1942 the Japanese occupied the Indies, defeating the colonial army and imprisoning the Dutch under harsh conditions. On 17 August 1945, following Japan's defeat in World War Ⅱ, Indonesian nationalists led by Sukarno and Mohammad Hatta declared Indonesian independence. The Dutch did not accept and for five years fought the new republic, mainly in Java. Indonesian independence was established in 1950.

As in many developing countries, Indonesia's population is still a young one. Population has grown at different rates in different areas owing to such factors as economic conditions and standard of living, nutrition, availability and effectiveness of public health and family planning programs, and cultural values and practices. Migration also plays a part in population fluctuations. Increased permanent or seasonal migration to cities accompanied economic development during the 1980s and 1990s, but there is also significant migration between rural areas as people leave places such as South Sulawesi for more productive work or farm opportunities in Central Sumatra or East Kalimantan.

Exercises

Task 1 Decide whether the following sentences are True or False.

1. The name Indonesia, meaning Indian Islands, was coined by a German geographer. ( )
2. The archipelago's location has played a profound role in economic, political, cultural, and religious developments there. ( )
3. There are some four hundred active volcanoes in Indonesia. ( )

4. About 200 C.E., small states that were deeply influenced by Chinese civilization began to develop in Southeast Asia, primarily at estuaries of major rivers. (　　)
5. People only migrate from rural areas to cities. (　　)

Task 2 Answer the following questions according to the information from text A.

1. What does the underlined sentence mean in paragraph 3?

____

____

2. What good does the volcanic lava and ash do to the agriculture?

____

____

3. What are the prominent plantation-grown products in Sumatra and Java?

____

____

4. How did the Netherlands Indies government extend its authority to all of present Indonesia at the beginning of the twentieth century?

____

____

5. Why has population grown at different rates in different areas?

____

____

Task 3 Translate the following sentences into Chinese.

1. For more than two thousand years, trading ships sailed between the great civilizations of India and China via the waters and islands of the Indies.

____

____

2. Numerous rivers flowing from mountainous or jungle interiors to coastal plains and ports have carried farm and forest products for centuries and have been channels for cultural

communication.

____

____

3. Sporadic nineteenth century revolts against Dutch practices occurred mainly in Java, but it was in the early twentieth century that Indonesian intellectual and religious leaders began to seek national independence.

____

____

Task 4 Critical thinking enhancement.

The Organization of the Petroleum Exporting Countries (OPEC) was founded in Baghdad, Iraq, with the signing of an agreement in September 1960 by five countries namely Islamic Republic of Iran, Iraq, Kuwait, Saudi Arabia and Venezuela (Founder Members of the Organization). Indonesia joined OPEC in 1962, suspended its membership in January 2009, reactivated it again in January 2016, and decided to suspend its membership once more at the 171st Meeting of the OPEC Conference on 30 November 2016. Try to find some reasons why Indonesia suspended its membership in 2016.

____

____

____

____

____

Text B

The Diversity of Malaysia[①]

The country of Malaysia, located in Southeast Asia, is an incredible mixing pot of cultures. Bordering everything from Thailand and the South China Sea to Brunei and Indonesia, Malaysia has a central location that shouldn't be skipped when exploring Southeast Asia.

Cultures have been meeting and mixing in Malaysia since the very beginning of its history. More than fifteen hundred years ago a Malay kingdom in Bujang Valley welcomed traders from China and India. With the arrival of gold and silks, Buddhism and Hinduism also came to Malaysia. A thousand years later, Arab traders arrived in Malacca and brought with them the principles and practices of Islam. By the time the Portuguese arrived in Malaysia, the empire that they encountered was more cosmopolitan than their own.

Malaysia's cultural mosaic is marked by many different cultures, but several in particular have had especially lasting influence on the country. Chief among these is the ancient Malay culture, and the cultures of Malaysia's two most prominent trading partners throughout history — the Chinese, and the Indians. These three groups are joined by a dizzying array of indigenous tribes, many of which live in the forests and coastal areas of Borneo. Although each of these cultures has vigorously maintained its traditions and community structures, they have also blended together to create contemporary Malaysia's uniquely diverse heritage.

One example of the complexity with which Malaysia's immigrant populations have contributed to the nation's culture as a whole is the history of Chinese immigrants. The first Chinese to settle in the straits, primarily in and around Malacca, gradually adopted elements of Malaysian culture and intermarried with the Malaysian community. Known as babas and nonyas, they eventually produced a synthetic set of practices, beliefs, and arts, combining Malay and Chinese traditions in such a way as to create a new culture. Later Chinese, coming to exploit the tin and rubber booms, have preserved their culture much more meticulously. A city like Penang, for example, can often give one the impression of being in China rather than in Malaysia.

Another example of Malaysia's extraordinary cultural exchange is the Malay wedding ceremony, which incorporates elements of the Hindu traditions of southern India: The bride and groom dress in gorgeous brocades, sit in state, and feed each other yellow rice with hands painted with henna. Muslims have adapted the Chinese custom of giving little red packets of

---

① Kaleideculture. [2022-05-09]. http://www.geographia.com/malaysia/cultures.html.
10 Top Reasons Why You Should Visit Malaysia. (2020-09-07) [2022-05-10]. http://www.touropia.com/reasons-to-visit-malaysia/.

money (Ang Pau) at festivals to their own needs; the packets given on Muslim holidays are green and have Arab writing on them.

You can go from a Malaysian kampung to a rubber plantation worked by Indians to Penang's Chinese Kongsi and feel you've traveled through three nations. But in cities like Kuala Lumpur, you'll find everyone in a grand melange. In one house, a Chinese opera will be playing on the radio; in another they're preparing for Muslim prayers; in the next, the daughter of the household readies herself for classical Indian dance lessons.

Perhaps the easiest way to begin to understand the highly complex cultural interaction is to look at the open door policy maintained during religious festivals. Although Malaysia's different cultural traditions are frequently maintained by seemingly self-contained ethnic communities, all of Malaysia's communities open their doors to members of other cultures during a religious festival — to tourists as well as neighbors. Such inclusiveness is more than just a way to break down cultural barriers and foster understanding. It is a positive celebration of a tradition of tolerance that has for millennia formed the basis of Malaysia's progress.

The diversity of Malaysia could be better experienced when you travel there. In the same country, you can explore thriving, modern cities, and colonial architecture, relax on some of the most beautiful beaches on the planet and hike through lush green jungles. Here are just some of the top reasons to visit Malaysia on your next trip.

Architecture

The city of Kuala Lumpur is a fantastic place to admire the more modern architecture in Malaysia, and in particular the contemporary skyscrapers that create one of Asia's most iconic skylines. If possible, take time to see the Petronas Twin Towers in the district known as the Golden Triangle. Once the tallest buildings in the world, and now connected by a skybridge, the Petronas Twin Towers are just a short walk from other incredible structures like the KL Tower and its viewing deck.

With Malaysia's long colonial history, it boasts an array of colonial architecture. If you're interested in this blast from the past, there can be no better spot to visit than Melaka. The city has been ruled by the British, the Dutch and the Portuguese, and its architecture reflects that. Just some of the buildings you can explore include the ruins of a 16th century Portuguese fortress, the oldest Protestant church in Malaysia and the Stadthuys Town Hall, which still stands as the oldest as well as the largest Dutch colonial building in the region.

Chinatowns

Malaysia has been influenced by cultures from around the globe. Proximity to China means that Malaysia is home to excellent Chinese cuisine and a vibrant heritage. You can experience this influence first hand by exploring one of the Chinatowns in Malaysia, the largest of which is in George Town. In this Chinatown, you can see a 200-year-old Kuan Yin Teng Temple or indulge in the local street fare. Don't miss dining at one of the local dim sum restaurants or trying the hot egg waffles sold from vendors right on the street.

Tea plantations

The tea industry has long been a part of development and trade in Malaysia, particularly in areas like the Cameron Highlands. There, near the highest point of the country, temperatures are cool enough for tea plantations. In the Cameron Highlands, you can take a guided tour of the nation's largest tea company, hike through the plantation itself or sip local teas at some of the smaller plantations in the vicinity.

Hiking

Hiking may not be the first thing that comes to mind when thinking about Malaysia, but the country actually boasts a number of excellent hiking spots. None, however, can compare to Mount Kinabalu. In the state of Sabah, Mount Kinabalu boasts miles of hiking trails that pass through six distinct vegetation zones at varying elevations. To climb the entire summit, expect to spend two days hiking with a night of camping in between.

Diving

One of the most popular reasons to visit Malaysia is for the chance to go diving. Just off the tip of Malaysian Borneo is Sipidan, known as one of the world's best dive sites. Diving in Sipidan's protected waters is limited to just a set number of people each day, and it provides the chance to see things like turtles, barracudas, sharks and parrotfish. If you can't make it to Sipidan, islands like Redang and Tioman are also excellent, although their diving seasons are more limited.

Wildlife

Much of Malaysia is undeveloped, allowing wildlife to roam freely. One of the top spots to admire wildlife in its natural habitat is in Taman Negara National Park. Among waterfalls and canopy walks, you can spot tapirs, wild boar, deer, monkey and countless birds and insects. In Borneo, you may be able to see even bigger animals, and guided tours can get you up close and personal with the likes of elephants, tigers, rhinos and orangutans.

Beaches and islands

Malaysia is a tropical country with a warm climate and miles of coastline, so it should come as no surprise that beaches are plentiful. While there are excellent beaches on the mainland, it is Malaysia's islands that are the most popular for beach lovers. Langkawi is the ultimate spot for a relaxing beach vacation, complete with shopping and dining. If you're after a more secluded, less touristy getaway, Redang is a pristine island that also serves as a turtle sanctuary.

Caves

In Sarawak, on the island of Borneo, is Gunung Mulu National Park. This park has a history dating back for more than 3,000 years, and it is best known for its incredible caverns. On guided tours, you can explore Turtle Cave, the so-called Garden of Eden or the Wind Caves, all of which are in the park. Some caves require you to bring flashlights, but others are simple strolls in incredible environments. If you're staying closer to Kuala Lumpur, you can set off on a day trip to the Batu Caves, which are made from limestone and offer some challenging hikes as well as amazing scenery.

Exercises

Task 1 Use the proper forms of the words in the table to complete the following sentences. You may not use any of the words in the table more than once.

vigorously	indulge	synthetic	indigenous	boast
incredible	meticulously	incorporate	ultimate	roam

1. She does not believe in ________ the children with presents.
2. Scientists have more to do than to allow their imaginations to ________ at large.
3. We have ________ all the latest safety features into the design.
4. This race will be the ________ test of your skill.
5. African dance is ________, but full of subtlety.
6. Speak little of your ill luck and ________ not of your good luck.
7. He's always ________ in keeping the records up to date.
8. Each country has its own ________ cultural tradition.
9. Some planets run at ________ speed.
10. With quality grade of the lubricating oils is improved, ________ oils are more and more used.

Task 2 Answer the following questions according to the information from text B.

1. What cultures in particular have had especially lasting influence on Malaysia?

____

____

2. Which countries once colonized the Melaka city?

____

____

3. What may be the easiest way to begin to understand the highly complex cultural interaction?

____

____

Task 3 Translate the following sentences into Chinese.

1. Although each of these cultures has vigorously maintained its traditions and community structures, they have also blended together to create contemporary Malaysia's uniquely diverse heritage.

____

____

2. Proximity to China means that Malaysia is home to excellent Chinese cuisine and a vibrant heritage.

____

____

3. Malaysia is a tropical country with a warm climate and miles of coastline, so it should come as no surprise that beaches are plentiful.

____

____

Task 4 Please write an essay of 300 words in response to the following question.

Malaysia is a country that celebrates its diversity. Whereas in some other countries there is a trend towards creating a homogeneous society for the purpose of national unity, in Malaysia the various races are encouraged to keep their ethnic names and their languages, to practice their respective religions and to embrace not only their own cultures, but fellow citizens'. All this has served to create a vibrant multi-cultural society.

A homogeneous society or a vibrant multi-cultural society, which do you prefer and why?

____

____

____

____

____

Text C

Confucianism in Vietnam①

Confucianism in Vietnam can be considered as a social philosophy than just a normal religion. It has no church, no clergy and no bible as well. It advocates a code of social behavior that man ought to live in harmony with society and attain happiness in his individual life.

Confucianism was introduced into Vietnam early during the Chinese rule and has maintained its influence since that time. In 1072, there was a temple dedicated to Confucius and his leading 72 disciples. Located in Hanoi, this temple was called the Temple of Literature. If one of you has ever been to Saigon, you can see at the Botanical Gardens a temple dedicated to Confucius. This is the site of Confucius' birthday celebration which is solemnly honored each year.

As a major emphasis in its ethical system, Confucianism regulates relations between people. If there is improper conduct of these relations, it will cause disorders in the social group and therefore, throw man out of harmony with the universe. The cosmic world (heaven and earth) are in harmony and man's aim is to achieve a similar one. Vietnamese Confucianism, though without a strong formalized organization, still vitally affects nearly all ethnic Vietnamese. This is part of the cultural environment where the child is born.

The profound impact of Confucianism remains strong in Vietnam. Social order is defined by its principle as well as the rituals, deference and obedience.

Confucianism gave Vietnam a highly organized hierarchical society. Yet, while encouraging the improvement of the individual, it did also appeal his positive relationship with the community. In this sense, Confucianism is anti-individualistic.

According to Confucianism, death does not mean the annihilation of man. Confucianists believe that, the spirit which wanders in space as an exile should be brought back to the family altar and be worshiped. Besides, filial reverence is the primary duty of all Confucianists. That is why, on all solemn occasions, the ancestral spirit is invoked and offered liquors, flowers and fruit, accompanied with prayers and incense.

Confucianism is vividly seen throughout Vietnam in the Festival of the Arrival of Spring, the Mid-Autumn Festival, the Children's Festival and the Festival of Tet. Tet is the festival of renewal and rebirth, or meditation and hope. With fireworks, ringing bells, beating tom-toms, toys and food, Tet is a big occasion in Vietnam. Many folk visit the pagodas to worship, burn

① TRAN R. Confucianism in Vietnam. (2020-02-06) [2022-06-30]. https://vietnamdiscovery.com/culture-arts/confucianism-in-vietnam/.

joss-sticks and sandalwood incense, with flowers, food and liquors placed also on the family altars.

The other worship occasions involve the worship of the land. Such ceremonies include the Festival of the Beginning of Plowing, the Rice Festival, the Harvest Festival and the Festival of the First Fruits. In spite of drought, war, floods... the Vietnamese farmers never seem to lose faith in the land as they plow, plant, harrow, weed and irrigate it. To express their thankfulness, the land is given honor in seasonal festivals. Such worship of the land has tended to create in the Vietnamese peasant an almost fanatical attachment to his birthplace which nourished him during his life. It is the combination of worship of the land and ancestor veneration that creates the sight of numberless graves being scattered throughout the farming areas of Vietnam.

Besides, Confucianism has exercised a powerful influence in the formation of Vietnamese society where family is the basic unit. Thus, the three fundamental principles which govern Vietnamese women are the obedience to father until married, the obedience to husband while married, the obedience to eldest son when husband is dead.

However, the value of Confucianism as a moderating influence upon social behavior is being rapidly superseded by the flexibility and openness in a developing society.

Exercises

Task 1 Answer the following questions according to the information from text C.

1. What is the role of Confucianism in the Vietnamese ethical system?

____

____

2. Why does the author think that Confucianism is anti-individualistic?

____

____

3. What are the worship occasions mentioned in the text?

____

____

Task 2 Translate the following sentences into Chinese.

1. Confucianism gave Vietnam a highly organized hierarchical society. Yet, while encouraging

the improvement of the individual, it did also appeal his positive relationship with the community.

____

____

2. It is the combination of worship of the land and ancestor veneration that creates the sight of numberless graves being scattered throughout the farming areas of Vietnam.

____

____

3. Confucianism has exercised a powerful influence in the formation of Vietnamese society where family is the basic unit.

____

____

Task 3 Expanded learning: *Vietnam from Above*.①

The documentary *Vietnam from Above* guides us to travel across Vietnam on a breathtaking cultural and historical journey. It uncovers ancient Chinese influences on Vietnamese traditions and striking examples of French colonial architecture, and traces the impact of the Vietnam War in the north and south. The country's lively modern cities, temples, floating markets, and the world heritage sites are all visited.

____

____

____

____

____

① The video can be accessed here: https://www.bilibili.com/bangumi/play/ep282893?spm_id_from=333.337.0.0.

Practical Tips

Wisdom from Southeast Asia①

Everything is different in Southeast Asia — the sights, the smells and the people. Henry Miller once said, "One's destination is never a place, but a new way of seeing things." I recently returned from a whirlwind tour of Southeast Asia and, because of it, see the world differently. The magic of travel is that you leave the security of your home and the known and enter a world you cannot imagine or derive from any book. We open ourselves to the unknown and realize that the world is both big and small all at once. We become different — better versions of ourselves. As I traveled in Southeast Asia, I took away wisdom from each country I visited and that has given me a "new way of seeing things".

Singapore and diversity

Once a trading post for the East India Company, Singapore has been the center of business in Southeast Asia ever since. Its socially progressive policies and acceptance of diversity have led the World Bank to consistently name it the "Easiest Place to Do Business". Ranked 11th globally on the UN's Human Development Index, 90 percent of citizens own homes. Lacking natural resources, though, it has chosen to focus on its talent resources to build a knowledge economy. Forty-seven percent of citizens go on to post-secondary education, and the country has a goal of being a "global schoolhouse" attracting first-class universities, including Duke, MIT, and INSEAD. While crisscrossing Singapore on its easy-to-navigate public transportation, I saw a true melting pot, that is building a thriving economy by choosing diversity as a prized possession.

Vietnam and persistence

Vietnam has been one of the most prized territories in Southeast Asia, but it has emerged as a thriving independent economy with one of the highest growth rates in the world. Although still largely an agrarian economy, it is making economic gains in high-tech and manufacturing industries. These gains have largely reversed its poverty rate and greatly improved living standards, especially in rural communities. What struck me about Vietnam is the persistence of its people to improve their lives and their community. When we toured the coastal town of Phu My, women on motorbikes persistently followed us to sell their handmade crafts. By the end,

① SMITH S. Wisdom from Southeast Asia. (2016-08-17) [2022-05-22]. https://socialimpactarchitects.com/wisdom-from-southeast-asia/.

I was compelled to buy a number of souvenirs just to reward their efforts. Its culture values harmony and humanity, which in combination, has led it to progress swiftly as a country and a leader in Southeast Asia.

Cambodia and gratitude

Cambodia is a beautiful country with even more beautiful people. To Western eyes, this country has a long way to go toward curbing widespread poverty, low human development and corruption. Yet, the Cambodian people, where 95 percent practice Buddhism and believe in the importance of bonn (merit) and good karma (work), exude gratitude. When I toured a school in Sihanoukville, I encountered curious children excited to meet an American and anxious to speak English. Cambodia is a land of untapped potential, and I look forward to seeing how it harnesses its human potential for future growth.

Thailand and inner peace

I enjoyed the unique juxtaposition of the energetic flow of Bangkok streets with the peaceful serenity of its temples. And, the Thai people make this dichotomy work. When visiting Wat Ratchanatdaram, one of the famous Buddhist temples in the heart of Bangkok, I found a meditation that gave me insight into their culture: "By not being angered by someone who is angry, you have won the battle not easily won." It reminds me that the battle is not an external one at all, but an internal one. The key isn't the absence of conflict in life, but maintaining control and a peaceful heart in the face of conflict.

Each country opened up my eyes to new ways of seeing the world and myself as well as the importance of having values that drive our efforts and culture. Diversity. Persistence. Gratitude. Inner Peace. I came back from vacation refreshed, but also reinvigorated with new wisdom to add to my daily practice and my work with clients. Southeast Asia is an amazing place with a lot to teach all of us.